"THE LIVING CHURCH" SERIES

Edited by

Professor JOHN E. McFADYEN, D.D.

United Free Church College, Glasgow.

Crown 8vo, cloth boards, 6s. net per volume.

IT has of late become the fashion to belittle the Church as of negligible importance in the affairs of the great world. Those alike who love and who deride her often little understand how great has been her influence in the past, and how much she has done, in many departments of thought and activity, for the higher life of the world. The aim of *The Living Church* Series is partly historical, partly practical : it is to help people to realise what a tremendous factor the Church has been in history, and to show how in fresh forms the old needs, problems, and tasks are perpetually re-emerging—in short, to stimulate a fresh appreciation of the Church and to quicken faith in her power to affect the future as she has affected the past.

The following volumes have been arranged for :

*The Changing Church and the Unchanging Christ.
By R. H. COATS, B.D., Birmingham.

*The Christian Church and Liberty. (4s. 6d. net.)
By A. J. CARLYLE, M.A., D.LITT., Oxford.

The Church and Art.
By J. ROBERTSON CAMERON, PH.D., Aberdeen.

The Church and the Bible.
By PROF. WILLIAM A. CURTIS, D.LITT., D.D., Edinburgh.

The Church's Charter.
By PROF. JOSEPH F. McFADYEN, M.A., D.D., Kingston, Ontario.

*The Church and the Creeds.
By DANIEL LAMONT, B.D., Helensburgh.

*The Church's Debt to Heretics.
By PROF. RUFUS M. JONES, D.D., Haverford, Pa., U.S.A.

The Church and Education.
By PROF. ARCH. MAIN, D.LITT., D.D., Glasgow

The Church and the Healing Ministry.
> By Prof. Samuel McComb, D.D., Cambridge, Mass., U.S.A., and Elwood Worcester, D.D., Boston, U.S.A.

The Church and the Hymn Writers.
> By G. Currie Martin, M.A., B.D., London.

The Church and Literature.
> By John A. Hutton, D.D., London.

*The Church and Missions.
> By Robert E. Speer, D.D., LL.D., New York, U.S.A.

*The Church at Prayer.
> By Prof. Percy Dearmer, M.A., D.D., London.

*The Church and the Sacraments.
> By Principal W. M. Clow, D.D., Glasgow.

The Church and Science.
> By Hector Macpherson, M.A., Ph.D., F.R.A.S., F.R.S.E., Edinburgh.

*The Church and the Sex Question.
> By J. W. Coutts, M.A., Milngavie.

The Church and the State.
> By Prof. P. Carnegie Simpson, D.D., Cambridge.

*The Church and Woman.
> By A. Maude Royden, London.

Current Cults.
> By Prof. R. E. Welsh, D.D., Montreal.

*The Mystics of the Church.
> By Evelyn Underhill, London.

*The One Body and the One Spirit.
> By Canon T. A. Lacey, M.A., Worcester.

*The Preachers of the Church.
> By Principal A. E. Garvie, D.D., London.

Representative Churchmen of Twenty Centuries.
> By Prof. Hugh Watt, B.D., Edinburgh.

*The Story of Social Christianity (2 vols.).
> By F. Herbert Stead, M.A., Warden of Browning Hall, 1894-1921.

*The Thinkers of the Church.
> By Arch. B. D. Alexander, D.D., Langbank.

*The Vocation of the Church.
> By J. H. Leckie, D.D., Edinburgh.

The volumes marked with an asterisk are now ready.

JAMES CLARKE & CO., Ltd., 9 Essex Street, Strand, London, W.C.2

THE PREACHERS OF THE CHURCH

THE PREACHERS
OF THE CHURCH

BY

ALFRED ERNEST GARVIE

M.A. (Oxon.), D.D. (Glas.)

PRINCIPAL OF HACKNEY AND NEW COLLEGE, LONDON

Author of

"A GUIDE TO PREACHERS," "THE CHRISTIAN PREACHER," ETC.

"I came to Irvine, and heard a well-favoured, proper old man (David Dickson) with a long beard, and that man showed me all my heart. Then I went to St. Andrews, where I heard a sweet majestic-looking man (R. Blair), and he showed me the majesty of God. After him I heard a little fair man (Rutherford) and he showed me the loveliness of Christ."

An English Merchant visiting Scotland.

LONDON

JAMES CLARKE & CO., LIMITED

9 ESSEX STREET, STRAND, W.C.2

"THE LIVING CHURCH" SERIES

Printed in Great Britain

To

THE SACRED MEMORY

OF

WALTER C. SMITH, D.D.

AND OF

NEWMAN SMYTH, D.D.

PIONEERS IN FRESH PATHS OF CHRISTIAN TRUTH

IN GRATEFUL ACKNOWLEDGMENT OF A

GREAT DEBT

PREFACE

In preparing this volume I have yielded, I trust not unwisely, to the desire of my friend, the Editor of this series, the Rev. Dr. McFadyen. The title of the series, " The Living Church," also attracted me, as I was persuaded that things worth saying might be said to show how the Church can live in its preachers. This has been throughout my guiding thought. I have already written two volumes on preaching, *A Guide to Preachers*, which was intended only for local preachers, but in which many ministers have found practical guidance, and *The Christian Preacher*, the greater part of which was concerned with the history of preaching, but which also discussed the varied aspects of the preacher's work, and offered an exposition of homiletics, the theory of preaching. It will be impossible in this volume not to stray sometimes into the same fields of knowledge and judgment; but the distinctive purpose and the different method here will, it is hoped, save from all vain repetition, and present the subject of preaching under fresh aspects. If this volume serves in any way to encourage and help my brothers in the ministry of the

Gospel, I shall feel myself richly repaid for any labour I have put into it. May the Living Lord Himself through it impart His truth and grace to those whom He has called to set forth His unsearchable riches !

I am deeply indebted to my elder daughter for typewriting the whole MS.

ALFRED E. GARVIE

New College, London.
May 5th, 1926.

CONTENTS

CONTENTS

PART II. PRACTICAL COUNSELS

INTRODUCTION

THE LIVING CHURCH AND ITS PREACHERS

THE purpose of this volume is determined by the title of the series to which it belongs. It is concerned with the nature of the Living Church, and the function within it that the preachers fulfil. The three questions to which in this Introduction we must address ourselves are:

(1) What is the Church?
(2) What makes it Living?
(3) How can preachers express, sustain, and develop that Life?

(I) The Church is not any ecclesiastical organization or social institution of man's devising and founding.

(a) It is an ever-continued divine creation; it is the society of all who believe in Christ as Saviour and Lord, and possess the Spirit of God. It is by the divine impartation of grace and the human reception of that grace in faith that the Church is ever being 'new created.' By faith believers are so closely united to Christ as to become members of His body, partakers of His life (as the branches

13

in the Vine); as that life by His Spirit or the Spirit of God is their *common possession*, they become members of one another in their mutual fellowship, and are thus the *community* (koinoñia) of the Spirit. As the body of Christ and the community of the Spirit they are also being built up together into the holy temple of God, where the glory of His Presence is made manifest. This is the New Testament ideal, and by it the historical actuality must be judged, and to it it must be conformed.

(*b*) As there is one God and Father of all, one Saviour and Lord of all, one Spirit of God in all, the Church is *one*, and cannot but be *one*. This is the dominant note of the New Testament, and in so far as Protestantism has ignored that unity, it is wrong, and Catholicism in emphasizing that unity is right, although mistaken in identifying that unity with uniformity of polity, creed, or ritual. The use of the term *church* for the local congregation in the New Testament can be explained only because the local congregation was for faith the local manifestation and activity of the *one Church*. The believers as already members of the body of Christ gave to that body "a local habitation and a name," when in the name of Christ they gathered together for worship, witness, and work. The New Testament happily knows nothing of the use of the name *Church* for a denomination, as despite the occasions for division, schism was avoided by the guidance of the Spirit. The use of the term can, however, be justified on the ground that the denomination, if it indeed preserves the truth and the grace of

14

Christ, is an expression, even if partial, of the one Church, which the historical conditions may have demanded, and may have justified. But admitting the legitimacy of the use of the term *church* in these two senses, it is disastrous, when either the local congregation, or the partial denomination, is allowed to displace from the forefront of esteem, interest, and purpose the Church as by its very nature *one*.

(*c*) The Church is a spiritual society, an object of faith, and not of sense; for it is by faith and faith only believers know themselves to be members of Christ's body, and members of one another in that body, possessors of the Spirit of God in common with other believers, and so becoming parts of the temple of God. The spiritual society must, however, become sensibly manifest if it is to discharge its mission, and deliver its message in the world. As the soul needs the body, so inspiration needs organization to be effective. From the very beginning the Christian Church has been a visible association in the world with varied and varying forms of organization adapted in the existing conditions for the fulfilment of its purpose in the world. What has to be avoided on the one hand is such an identification of the invisible society and the visible association as to ignore the difference which in human affairs exists between the ideal and the actual; and on the other such a separation as leaves the invisible society as an impotent abstraction, and the visible association as the only effective actuality. The ideal must be actualized, even if imperfectly, and the actuality must ever be referred for judgment to the ideal. The spiritual society must become manifest in the sensible organization, and that organization must be conformed as far as possible, to the society.

(d) As in an organism there are different organs for the discharge of different functions in the vital process, so within the organization of the Christian Church there are different ministries. The assumption of the New Testament is that all the members of the Church will also be ministers, each exercising for the common good the gifts of the Spirit which each may possess, for the possession of a gift implies the obligation of its use in the service of the community of the Spirit. But in the New Testament already there is implicit the distinction between what may be called *individual* and what may be described as *corporate* ministries. The Church as a unity was represented by apostles, prophets, evangelists, teachers, the local congregation by presbyters or bishops, and deacons. The inspiration of the one class so authenticated their ministry that no ordination was needed; the others, although their gifts were also recognized as from the Spirit, were ordained to discharge a representative office in the local administration. Gradually the functions of the first class passed over to the second; the itinerant universal ministry was superseded by the settled local ministry. Without now entering on the disputed questions about the development of the threefold ministry of bishops, elders, and deacons during the first three centuries, it is enough

16

INTRODUCTION

for the present purpose to establish the fact that some form of ordained ministry has belonged to the Christian Church from its beginnings. The minister is not an individual believer voluntarily and occasionally using his special gift for the common good, but a representative person, discharging in a life-long vocation corporate functions for the community of believers.

(e) This conception needs to be emphasized, as among some sections of English Nonconformity there is a tendency, while maintaining an ordained ministry, to ignore or even deny its distinctive position within the Church. It is assumed that no man chooses the ministry as he might another profession; but that he is conscious of a divine call to dedicate his whole life to this vocation. He receives the educational equipment which is regarded as necessary for the efficient discharge of his function; his qualifications, intellectual, moral and spiritual are scrutinized by the appropriate authority in the denomination in which he desires to exercise his Christian ministry. His inward call from God must be confirmed by the outward call of the Church, whether it be a local congregation or a denomination. He is ordained; he dedicates himself, and is dedicated by the Church, to his life-long vocation, with the invocation of the divine blessing on that dedication. He is not, therefore, one of the members of the church merely, paid to give all his time to work that others might do just as well; he is the representative person in the church, which has called him to be its minister, and he discharges the corporate functions of the church which he thus represents. What he does is for the Church, and the Church acts in the matters entrusted to him, through him. As representative he is dependent on, and responsible to the church as a community of the Spirit, but not an underling of any individual member. He has, however, the dignity of the representative member through whom the church discharges its corporate functions. This view is neither sacerdotal nor hierarchical; but it does assert the distinctive position of the minister within the Church.

(*f*) What then are the corporate functions which as the representative person the minister discharges in the name and on behalf of the Church ? The Protestant Confessions usually mention two, the preaching of the Gospel, and the administration of the Sacraments, and some add a third, the exercise of discipline over the individual members. It was in the Reformed or Calvinistic churches, which regarded the Bible as a code of law, divinely given, that emphasis was laid upon discipline; it was not so in the Evangelical or Lutheran churches. Catholicism, Anglican as well as Roman, has tended to lay more stress on the administration of the Sacraments, and Protestantism on the preaching of the Gospel. I have no hesitation in giving the first place in the functions of the Church, and so of the Ministry, to the preaching of the Gospel, and that for three reasons.

(i) All the religions which have had a historical founder have been begun, carried on, and spread abroad by the proclamation in informal conversation or formal discourse of the message which the founder believed he had to deliver to the world. Confucius, Gautama the Buddha, and Mohammed were teachers or preachers. Jesus went about delivering the Gospel of the Kingdom of God; and the Gospel of Christ as Saviour and Lord was spread throughout the world by apostles, prophets, evangelists, teachers. It is through speech that men most fully and freely communicate with one another, and it is through speech that God communicates His mind, heart, and will by men whom His Spirit has enlightened. As will be shown in a subsequent chapter, at the crises of the history of the Church, preaching has been a decisive factor.

(ii) There has been a tendency in recent years to magnify the influence of the subconscious in the religious life, and through the subconscious the influence of the other senses, sight, taste, smell, in contrast to hearing. In this way a support has been sought for sacramentalism, the belief in the conveyance of the divine grace by material channels other than the word spoken and heard. In its dread of superstition Protestantism has erred in ignoring as it has done the appeal to the emotions, the æsthetic sensibility, and the imagination by such means as the Catholic ritual may employ; and consistently with its own genius it might in some respects widen its influence. But it has not erred in its primary appeal to conscience and reason; and that appeal can be made most directly and effectively by speech. I believe that all this emphasis on the subconscious is a passing phase in psychology. The existence, the nature, and the function of the subconscious have to be inferred from the contents of consciousness, and the subconscious can be affected only by suggestions made to consciousness, and within consciousness. While we must avoid an intellectualism which divorces thought from feeling and deed, we must maintain the directive authority of the mind, whether theoretical, as in reason, or practical, as in conscience. Sacramentalists, when they depreciate preaching seem to forget that speech and hearing are both functions of the living organisms as is sight or taste or smell, and so divine grace is in it also being conveyed by material channels. Can it be denied that through speech personality can express itself in most cases more effectively than by any other means ?

(iii) Protestantism is right in subordinating the Sacraments to the Gospel as the signs, seals, and, where the human faith receives and responds to divine grace, even channels of the divine grace proclaimed in the Gospel. Had men not heard the Gospel, what meaning and what worth would the sacraments have ? Where an observance of Sacraments is detached from the preaching of the Gospel religion degenerates into superstition. Whatever mysterious virtue traditions and associations may attach to the sacraments, their efficacy as means of grace must surely depend on a knowledge of what the grace of God is, means, and does, such as only the preaching of the Gospel can impart. If Christ be not known, trusted, obeyed as Saviour and Lord,

what can Baptism or the Lord's Supper mean ?
To give the sacraments their full efficacy the Gospel
must be preached.

It is not less so with the discipline of the members
of the Church. Can a man be censured for doing
what his conscience has never been instructed to
condemn, or for failing to do what his conscience
has never learned to approve ? The standard of
judgment must be known if men are to be judged
by it. Not only this. Under modern conditions
there cannot be the exercise of discipline such as
used to be common. The moral guidance and
influence of the Church to-day must be exercised
through the pulpit. Alike as regards the means of
grace which the sacraments offer, or the standard
of duty to which believers may be expected
to conform, the preaching of the Gospel is
essential. It is, therefore, the primary function of
the Church.

II. Having discussed only in so far as the present
purpose required the nature of the Church, we have
next to enquire when does it deserve to be called
Living ?

(*a*) The term itself suggests and even justifies
a biological analogy. An organism preserves its
own type in its development, but for self-preservation
it must ever be adjusting itself to its environment.
It is affected by its environment, but it may react
on its environment; e.g., the presence of the trees
has an effect on the climate of the country, in regard
to its moisture, the amount of rain: the earth-
worms change the nature of the soil. Where con-

sciousness emerges, and there is intelligent direction of the activities of the organism, the influence on the environment becomes greater. Man may more and more adjust his environment to himself, and himself less and less to his environment. What a change in the earth itself human culture and industry have effected ! An organism lives and grows as it adjusts itself to its environment, or its environment to itself; if it fails to do the one or the other it dies. This principle we can apply to the Church.

(*b*) The Church has a type of life to preserve; it would cease to be itself if it lost some of its distinctive features. We need not now discuss in detail what content of its thought, or what quality of its life is so essential to it that it would lose its identity if it lost the one or the other. Suffice it to urge that it is because Jesus Christ is " the same yesterday, to-day, yea and for ever," that there is a continuity in its thought and life, and that its distinctive type is preserved. In the historical reality of His revelation of God and His redemption of man there is the guarantee of its permanence. In the operation of His Spirit in ever re-interpreting and re-applying that reality amid changing conditions of thought and life is the assurance of its progress. As the to-day differs from yesterday, and the " for ever " will differ from to-day, so the Christ to be the same in His Saviourhood and Lordship must be presented in varying forms by His Spirit. There must be self-adaptation for self-preservation. Theology must change that the Gospel may remain the same; creeds, rituals, polities must be altered that the Church may survive.

(c) Hostile as at first sight the environment—the world—may appear to the organism—the Church; yet because the God who created the one is also the Creator of the other, there is affinity enough to allow not only the self-adjustment of the Church to the world, but the adjustment also of the world to the Church. The Church is so modifying the world as to make it an environment less alien and perilous to its life, and even as it makes the new environment, it must ever be adjusting itself afresh. It cannot affect a world by which it is not itself affected. The process of life demands "give and take," action and reaction in constant interchange. An insulated Church would be an impotent Church. The Church is living in the measure in which it is influencing and being influenced by the world. Its life is preserved by progress no less than per-manence.

(d) As Tennyson reminds us in his poem about "The flower in the crannied wall" the ultimate environment of even a plant is the Universe; but no organism relates itself directly to its whole environment. The fulness of the life of an organism, however, depends on the range of environment to which it relates itself; the wider its environment the richer is its life. The more points of contact it has with the world around, the more abundant content will it have in itself. Some living creatures relate themselves to their surroundings by an unconscious sensibility and mobility; man through his senses and by his movements relates himself in incalculable ways to the world around him. May we not then say that the Church will live most that relates itself most widely to the world ? The more numerous its points of contact are the more responsive will it be to the world around, and the more varied will be the influence that it can exert. As religion and morality are not departments of life but a quality which should belong to all life, a value which enhances all other values, so the Church must seek to relate itself as an organism, as an organ of religious and moral life, as far as possible, to the totality of its environment in the world. Much mischief has been done by too narrow an outlook upon the world, a detachment of the Church from many vital interests of humanity. Not only has society been less influenced than it might have been by the Church, but the development of the Church itself has been stunted. To the Church nothing human must be alien; it must extend the authority and influence of Christ into every sphere of human interest, activity, and relation.

(e) It must be admitted that the self-adaptation may go too far to be consistent with self-preservation. A man's body may adjust itself to certain industrial processes without any apparent immediate mischief, but an early breakdown or a shortening of life may be the result. Who can doubt that the Church has been at different periods of its history " secularized " in creed, ritual, and polity, and has lost some of its moral vigour and religious vitality ? But even as the body has in it reserves of life for recovery, so again and again the Church has been revived and reformed. It has resources that the physical organism cannot command. As long as it has faith and exercises that faith in prayer, it is in contact with the resources of God by His Spirit, and can be restored to its former fulness of life. Again and again, when the darkness of night seemed to be settling down on the Church, the dawn of a new day has broken upon it. The Church survives even its own faults and failures, because Christ lives, and renews its life in Him.

III. How can this life, self-preserving and self-adjusting, be expressed, sustained, and developed ?

(a) The life is expressed in the witness, the worship and the work of the Church, and by these means also is it sustained and developed. Moral and religious exercise is also the nourishment of the soul. As the Church expends its reserves of thought, feeling, and deed freely, so does it fully receive the resources of God. In spiritual reality possession is increased by expenditure. In prayer and praise the Church expresses its dependence and submission to God, and its gratitude and consecration to Him. The sacraments are the most permanent element in the worship of the Church; but in respect of one there has been self-adjustment. When the Church was at the beginning of its career, when it was still missionary, increasing its members by conversion, adult baptism was very properly the rule. At least there is no evidence in the New Testament of any child baptism. But when children were born and brought up in Christian homes and so received and responded to Christian influences from the earliest years, Infant Baptism came into use. In my judgment the change can be justified, although not the superstitious view of Baptismal Regeneration which attached itself to it. It was an instance of self-adaptation. If there are the two types of Christian experience, the definite conversion and the gradual development, it is right that these two types should be recognized in the rite of initiation.

(*b*) That it may do its work the Church must have an organization. In this matter too the Church has shown itself living in its self-adjustment. That Christ prescribed a polity for His Church is an assumption, of which the historical evidence in the New Testament is lacking, and which must rest on an inference from Patristic opinion in the second century. None of the recognized types of polity—episcopal, congregational, or presbyteral—can be found in the New Testament, although suggestions of them may be. We cannot say there was uniformity, but there was adaptation. Some Churches closely followed the Jewish synagogue, others the Gentile club in their congregational arrangements. I regard the emergence of the bishop out of the presbytery in the local Christian community, as a legitimate, because necessary, development. Apart from the extravagance of Ignatius' language, his contention for the unity of the Church under the authority of the bishop seems sound. Even the appeal of Irenæus to the bishop as custodian of the Apostolic doctrine, because the representative of an Apostolic Church, was in principle right (whether in each case the historical claim to be Apostolic could be made out is another matter). In the Cyprianic episcopate, however, it seems to me an alien—Jewish or pagan—element was introduced; this was a self-adjustment to the environment, which endangered the self-preservation of the organism.

(c) These two illustrations of the self-adjustment of the Church are the more instructive, as it is in ritual and in polity that the conservatism, which clings to religion more than morality, most asserts itself. In the doctrine of the Church there is likely to be more rapid and frequent change as the mind must always be adjusting itself to its intellectual environment, meeting new questions with fresh answers, responding in modifications of thought to the influence of growing knowledge. However much literalists and dogmatists may deceive themselves, " the faith once delivered to the saints " is not preserved by a mental stagnation, by a repetition of the same formulæ. Even when the same words are used, another meaning is put into them. For instance, what mental confusion is due to the retention of the term *person* in the doctrine of the Trinity, for it means to-day something different to those who are not familiar with its history than it meant to the framers of the creeds, and is more misleading for us than it was for them. On the contrary the word *person* in the doctrine of Christ is nearer the truth in its modern than its ancient use. If on so important, even crucial subjects, change of thought must be recognized, even where ecclesiastical conservatism has refused a change of terms, what doubt can there be that there is a constant self-adjustment going on in theology ? For many believers the change is without observation. It is the theologian who combines learning and insight, knowledge of what the past offers and of what the present needs, who consciously endeavours to make this self-adjustment as complete as it can be; and he is either condemned as a heretic, or accepted as a reformer.

(d) It is not an exaggeration to state that it is in *preaching* that this self-adjustment is likely to be most constant and direct. The man who is most fully endowed with the gifts that make the preacher great is himself a living man in living contact with the life that is around him. He is responsive to his hearers, and so receptive of the varied influences which are giving its distinctive character to his age. It may be even that he is impelled to become a preacher that he may impart to others the message God has entrusted to him. He reacts against his own time in its truths outworn, but acts upon his own time in the truth for which it craves; and his reaction and action are due to the activity of the Spirit of truth, whose function is to lead into " all the truth." He who speaks with authority is he on whom necessity to speak is laid. The earliest of the prophets discloses the secret of the preacher, who lives himself, and imparts life to others. " Surely the Lord God will do nothing, but He revealeth His secret unto His servants the prophets.

INTRODUCTION

The lion hath roared, who will not fear? the Lord
God hath spoken, who can but prophesy?"
(Amos iii, 7, 8.) There are two differences between
the Hebrew prophet and the Christian preacher,
which may appear to make the analogy less close.

(i) In the first place the prophet was an agent,
conscious of his inspiration, of a progressive
revelation of God. That revelation has been con-
summated in Christ, and beyond the Gospel of
His truth and grace there is no revelation. The
Christian preacher need not, however, only repeat
that Gospel in the same form of words. Men have
not discovered all its meaning, nor has that meaning
been fully disclosed in speech. The Spirit does not
supersede the revelation in Christ, but interprets
it for the thought, and applies it to the life of each
age. If the Christian preacher be not as conscious
of his individual inspiration as was the Hebrew
prophet; yet he can be conscious of belonging to a
community in whom the Spirit is the common
possession, in which he can in the measure of his
faith participate.

(ii) This leads us to the second difference. The
prophet spoke for God to the nation; he did not
speak for the nation. Usually his speech was a
condemnation of the life of the people, an offer of
judgment or mercy to the people. The Christian
preacher is, as has already been shown, a representative person discharging a corporate function of
the Church of Christ. What as such he is entitled
to speak must not only express his individual reason
and conscience, but also be in accord with the com-

29

mon convictions and aspirations of the religious community for which he speaks.

(*e*) The adjustment of the right of individual liberty, and of the claim of social responsibility is one of the most serious problems for the Christian preacher; and is one which at the present time is an ever pressing difficulty for many men.

(i) A man may solve the problem by separating himself from any religious community in order that he may be free to say whatever he believes that his reason or conscience requires him to say. As a rule such isolation results in growing eccentricity and ineffectiveness. The Christian religion is a religion of fellowship, and a man does not develop that personality which will be the best vehicle for the truth apart from a community. As this volume is concerned not with free lances but with the preachers of the Church, this instance need not concern us any further.

(ii) Even where a communion, such as the Baptist or Congregationalist, does not require subscription to a creed as a condition of ministry, but expects a personal confession of faith at ordination as a pledge of accord with what is generally believed among the Churches, absolute liberty of speech cannot be claimed. It is the community which gives the preacher his position of influence and authority, and he is under a moral and religious, if not legal, obligation not to preach another Gospel than that which is commonly held. My experience as a Christian minister among Congregationalists, with probably a wider range than a pastorate would give, convinces me that, except in those cases where the prejudices of a congregation may hamper the minister in his preaching, and they are not very common, the preacher has as much independence to preach what God bids him as he can reasonably desire, and that the great majority of preachers do not abuse the liberty which is granted to them. I am sure that the Gospel of the grace of God is as well preserved in these communions without a creed as in those where a creed is deemed necessary. Should a Congregational communion regard it as necessary to bear a common witness to Christian truth to meet a threatening challenge of it from without, or to exhibit the essential accord within, it has in the past made a declaration concerning the things most surely believed, but has never imposed it as a creed binding on the conscience of its ministers.

(iii) It is certain that not in the present nor probably in the future will any Church elaborate its authoritative theology, as in the Lutheran and Reformed Confessions of the sixteenth and seventeenth centuries. In proposals for Christian reunion what is usually suggested as the basis are the Apostolic and the Nicene creed. As historical monuments, expressing in the language of their day for the thought of their day the content of the objects of Christian faith, even a Congregationalist need not hesitate about giving them a place as indicating that continuity of the Church's faith throughout the centuries. Had I lived in the fourth century Athanasius and not Arius would have expressed the substance of the faith I hold now. Inadequate as the term *Homocusion* is for my philosophy, yet my theology is more in accord with that term than with any term which Arian or Semi-Arian used. As one who believes strongly in the continuity as well as the unity of the Christian Church, I should be quite prepared to use these creeds, just as I can use psalms and hymns, the theology of which I cannot accept literally, but the piety of which links me in fellowship with those who thus expressed what they believed. It does not seem to me at all impossible for a man to discover whether there is this continuity of faith between his theology to-day and the theology which creeds, psalms, or hymns express, whether he can candidly say what in his own thinking he believes to be the truth and can sincerely hold the creed as an expression of a living faith in fellowship with his own.

(iv) Having left Presbyterianism for Congregationalism because of my conscientious scruples about creed subscription, that is as far as I could for the sake of Christian reunion go; and preferring creed-free Congregationalism, I nevertheless try to be just to those who have subscribed a creed which it is certain they cannot hold literally. If in any community subscription is generally held to mean such literal acceptance, then a man for whom such a course is impossible should, if he is to preserve his honour, withdraw from it. I do not know any communion in which so oppressive an obligation is imposed. To impose it would be foolish and wicked tyranny. For *firstly* it is to misconceive the nature of religious truth, the finite expression of infinite reality, to suppose that it can be defined as can a command or prohibition in a legal instrument. The language of a creed must ever be symbolical, suggestive of more than words can express. *Secondly* it is to misconceive the relation of theology to faith as its intellectual expression, to assume that what is felt to be adequate for one age could be deemed equally adequate for another. The thoughts of men are widened and deepened with the process of the suns; knowledge grows, belief changes; and theology cannot be insulated. The words that express the truth for one age may suggest falsehood to another, for the meaning of language is always relative to the mental situation. He who does not accept a creed literally may be more faithful to its substance than the literalist is. I conclude that in an age of transition such as ours, charges of bad faith should not be made. The man who can conscientiously realize the continuity of his faith with the beliefs of the past, can sincerely interpret the articles of the creed of his communion in accord with what his thought to-day may demand. It is such loyalty of faith, and not acceptance of dogma, that is the condition of the continuity of the Church's witness.

(*f*) While the preacher must preach only what God gives him, and must seek to keep in living touch with the Christian community for which he speaks, it is his duty to be the voice of the Spirit of truth which is guiding not himself alone, but the whole Church into the truth. To solve the problem which has just been discussed by silence whenever speech might bring into conflict with ecclesiastical authority is not only to do injury to the individual conscience, but also to sacrifice the real interests of the Church. It is a vital interest of the Church, whether its rulers at the time recognize it or not, that it should be led by the Spirit of truth into the interpretations and applications of the Gospel which will answer the questions and meet the needs of the world, in which it is to bear its witness, and do its work. It is no less a vital interest that what it has apprehended of the things of God should be conveyed in the most persuasive and convincing presentation to the men who are outside of the Church because they have not found in it what they crave, the certainty of truth. The preacher must make the content of faith intelligible and credible to believers and unbelievers. It may be that one man as scholar and thinker can do the exploration in the regions beyond of the mystery of the Gospel, and that another may be alone fitted to report his results to others. Better is it when the preacher is himself scholar and thinker, for his study will be vitalized by his contact with men in preaching, and he who can report what he has himself discovered can speak with greater authority to others.

The purpose of this volume as stated in the preceding pages determines the method of treatment which will be adopted. Experience teaches, and counsels for the present need to be enforced by examples from the past. Accordingly in the first historical part of the volume illustrations will be given of the self-adjustment of the living Church to its environment at different periods, prophetic, apostolic, patristic, mediæval, reformation, revival, and missionary, and in the second or practical part the characteristics of the present environment of the preacher will be examined as the conditions of that self-adjustment, which the Church makes in the preachers.

PART I

HISTORICAL ILLUSTRATIONS

THE PREACHERS OF
THE CHURCH

CHAPTER I

THE PROPHETIC PERIOD

I. So closely is the New Testament related to the
Old, and the consummative revelation of God in
Christ to the progressive revelation in the *prophetic
succession*, that the Historical Illustrations must be
begun by a reference, though brief, to the ministry
of the prophets, as they were messengers of God,
each to his own age, with a distinctive message
determined by the circumstances and the events of
that age.

(1) Professor Theodore H. Robinson in his
book on *Prophecy and the Prophets* has insisted that
the Nabi' or " Ecstatic was the direct ancestor of the
Prophets whose words have been preserved for us
in the Old Testament." Although "the great
Canonical Prophets who followed them had a
message to deliver such as the world had never
heard before . . . men like Amos and Jeremiah
were not readily distinguished by their contem-
poraries from the Ecstatics whose symptoms

39

resembled those of the epileptic or even the insane."*
Their inspiration was authenticated for themselves
and for others by what we should now regard as
abnormal psychical conditions, visions, and voices.
The account Isaiah gives of his own call (Isaiah vi)
is not a literary invention, but presents an actual
experience, although literary art has been exercised
in the report of what he saw and heard. The
medium of communication is, however, less important than the certainty the prophet had of
speaking in the name and by the authority of God
a message from God to His people. The inspiration of the prophet in whatever form it came to
him did not suppress his personal activity; and the
prophetic writings display the characteristics of
the writer.

(2) The basis of the prophetic theology is found
in the earliest of the prophets whose writings have
come down to us. For Amos, Yahweh, the covenant
God, is the only God, because the only moral
authority, exercising judgment over other nations
besides Judah and Israel, and showing no partiality
in His judgment for His own covenant-people
(cc. i and ii). This "ethical monotheism" does
not rest on philosophical speculation as did such
monotheism as was reached by Plato or Aristotle,
but on moral conviction of the absolute value of
righteousness. In Isaiah xl. 4, it finds its triumphant and defiant exposition in contempt and
condemnation of polytheism and idolatry. Hosea,
the contemporary of Amos, emphasizes the love

* pp. 35-36.

of God, and consequently the mercy there is in His judgments. In their contrasts these two earliest prophets are typical of the succession in emphasizing either the righteousness or the mercy of God, His regard to the vindication of His own character, or His concern for the salvation of men. What is common to them all is the certainty that God is present and active in human history. This they do not state as an abstract theological proposition; but as acute observers of the events of their own time, they were also confident interpreters of the course of events as divine providence. Their message was always "up to date." It dealt with immediate dangers and duties, not with a remote future, but the future standing, as it were, and knocking at the door of the present. Theirs was a summons to penitence and reform to escape impending judgment, or to secure the swiftly passing mercy. How great was the significance that they attached to the present relation of God and His people is shown by their confident assertion, arrogant it would almost seem to be, that the great empires, Egypt, Assyria, Babylon, or Persia, were but instruments in God's hand in the fulfilment of His purpose in Israel or in Judah. We must not, however, charge them with a narrow nationalism, for contrary to the teaching of the " false " prophets, they were not concerned about any particular national interests, but about truth and righteousness, the holiness of God, and His people only as an instrument of His holy will. There are individual differences in the content and the emphasis of the messages, but what has been now stated is the common witness.

II. It is significant for the Christian preacher in many ways.

(1) He too should find God in human history present and active, not only in the history of the past, whether of the Hebrew nation, or of the Apostolic Age, but even in all the events of to-day; not in the domain of thought and life that as sacred is separated from the rest of man's interests, relations, and activities as secular, but in the whole course of history, for God is still fulfilling His purpose—the bringing of the Kingdom of God upon earth. In the fulfilment of that purpose nations no less than individuals have their divinely appointed tasks; for there is much in the interests of the Kingdom which could not be done by individual effort but which can be done by corporate. Not Assyria or Babylon alone can be the instruments of God, but France or Britain also. The Christian preacher can have a wider horizon than the Hebrew prophet, for all nations and people are now involved in one human destiny. He cannot in the same measure as did the Hebrew prophets concentrate his message on his own nation, and subordinate his interest in other peoples to his concern for his own. The whole world is now the scene of the divine drama of history; and events at the end of the earth are affecting the progress of the Kingdom of God. He must, however, recognize that it is in his own immediate surroundings that he can most effectively speak the word of God, and he must mainly address him-

self to his own people. As no society can rise above the level of its members, he will address himself to individuals, and will be concerned about their religious experience and moral character, but not primarily in view of their future destiny, now being determined, but in order that they may individually contribute their best now to the common good. The absence from the prophetic teaching of references to individual future destiny is significant, and is a corrective of the exaggerated individualism of the evangelical theology current during last century. The present and social reference of most of the prophetic utterances justifies the Christian preacher in avoiding as a hindrance to his discharge of his imperative duty the tendency to Apocalyptic interpretations which are in vogue in some circles, and in adhering to the vision and the summons which are expressed in the phrase " the coming of the Kingdom of God on earth." There is a purpose of God being fulfilled on earth, and the Christian preacher ought to be calling men to become fellow-workers with God in that fulfilment.

(2) A twofold objection may be offered to the Christian preacher's attempting to follow in the footsteps of the Hebrew prophet. On the one hand it may be pointed out how much folly has been shown in the attempts to foretell the future by the students of Apocalyptic literature, and on the other it may be urged that the Christian preacher lacks the distinctive endowment of the Hebrew prophet fo the interpretation of human history as divin providence.

43

(*a*) As regards the first objection the sufficient answer is that, as has just been indicated, the preacher should not find any present fulfilment of the Apocalyptic imagery, as Apocalypse relates to its own age, and can be intelligently interpreted only in relation to that age. Neither the book of Daniel nor the book of the Revelation has any reference to the history of this century; but the first relates only to the events of the second century B.C., and the second to the first century A.D. Apocalyptic speculation can only divert the Christian Church from its present opportunity and its imperative obligation.

(*b*) As regards the second objection it rests on two errors. In the first place it misconceives the character of the prophetic prediction, and in the second it ignores the quality of the Christian life.

(i) Prophecy is not history written beforehand, because man is a free agent in determining the course of history in so far as it depends on himself, and because God in controlling the course of that history has no rigid programme, but responds in His dealing with man to what man does. Accordingly all prediction is conditional. Threats of judgment heeded might avert the judgment; promises of mercy refused restrain the love of God. Some predictions were literally fulfilled, because the conditions of their fulfilment were actualized. The prophet's prediction was not based on a knowledge of the future supernaturally imparted, but on the foresight which his insight into the character and purpose of God gave him regarding

God's ways and works. It was as God's intimate, in moral and religious accord with God, that God's secret was disclosed to him. His predictions were not shrewd political guesses, although a knowledge of affairs was necessary to him that he might rightly read the signs of the times. They were the deliverances of a conscience made sensitive by communion with God. On such particular, definite prediction it is not desirable for the preacher to lay stress, as it was quite a subordinate element in the ministry of the prophet. In human history to-day there are too many factors involved for any preacher to command such a knowledge of them all as would justify him in confidently predicting the course of events. But his discernment, moral and religious, should enable him to declare with conviction what courses of individual action, national policy, or international relations are consistent with, and what contrary to the purpose of God for the common human good. He may not only state general principles, but may with care to be absolutely impartial, apply these principles to concrete instances. His main concern will be to imbue those who are practically engaged in any of these spheres of interest and activity in the world with these principles; but occasions may arise when he must unhesitatingly and yet considerately utter the Word of the Lord as he has apprehended it even as did the Hebrew prophet.

(ii) The quality of the Christian life makes a difference between the Hebrew prophet and the Christian preacher. The first stood alone, conscious of his individual inspiration. The second belongs to a society of which the Spirit of God is the common possession. Accordingly the Christian preacher will less rely on his own judgment, and be less ready to give his individual opinion than was the Hebrew prophet, conscious of his authority as God's messenger. The Christian preacher will rather in the fellowship of the saints, by conference with others, seek to discover what the Spirit of God is teaching the Churches, and to become one among other voices of a common judgment. An eccentric individualism in some who claimed to be following in the ways of the prophets has often brought discredit and even disaster. The Christian preacher may also be an inspired man, but not, as the Hebrew prophet must needs be, in individual isolation, but as possessing in common with other believers the gift of the Spirit of God. There have been periods in the history of the Church when a Christian preacher had to stand alone, as for instance Savonarola and Luther; and then he needed to have a confident conviction that God was calling him to the solitary and dangerous path. But to-day, so widespread is the desire to know, and the purpose to do what God requires, that His will may be done on earth as it is in heaven, that no preacher needs to separate himself from his fellows, and to expect a private revelation. His knowledge will be wider and his judgment surer as he seeks in fellowship with others to interpret his age according to God's mind.

(iii) There is a suggestive variant reading in

Romans xii, 11, serving the *Lord* or *occasion* (κυρίῳ καιρῷ) which has a lesson for us in this connection. While God is the *eternal* reality, yet He has a *temporal* purpose, in which He discloses His character in order that He may reproduce that character in men, and on this affinity of life may base community of love. God is served in *time*; he who understands aright the *occasion* will best fulfil the call of God. The Church best serves the eternal reality of God by making the most of the temporal occasion for the fulfilment of God's purpose in time. For this it needs not only an understanding of God, but also a knowledge of the occasion. In that knowledge and understanding it can confidently rely on the enlightening, quickening, and strengthening of the Spirit of God, for God does not repent of His gifts, and thus the holy enthusiasm and the holy energy of Pentecost can be renewed whenever and wherever there is faith to receive. The Christian preacher can claim to be in the prophetic succession as the representative person, discharging the corporate function of the Church of Christ, in declaring God's present summons to the immediate duty which the interpretation of human history as divine providence may indicate on each occasion.

CHAPTER II

THE APOSTOLIC PERIOD

GOD sent forth His Son in the fulness of the times. There had been a *praeparatio evangelica* such as Eusebius, the historian of the ancient Church, wrote about. Hebrew piety, Greek culture, and Roman government were the factors which made the environment congenial for the new life of the Christian Gospel. The adaptation was not so complete, however, that the new life had not to adjust itself to the surroundings. If we may recur to the biological analogy, when the chemical and physical conditions of the earth and its encompassing atmosphere were such that life could survive, life did appear. But the entire subsequent evolution of life was still a process of self-adjustment. Even so in the teaching of Our Lord there was adaptation to His hearers, although the adjustment was not so varied and extensive as it had to be when the Gospel was carried by the Apostle to the Gentile world. We may consider the preaching of the Apostolic Period in three stages, the teaching of Jesus, the preaching of the Church in the Jewish environment, the presentation of the Gospel, especially by Paul and in the Johannine literature, to the Gentile world.*

* See *The Christian Preacher*. Part I. Chapters I and II.

THE APOSTOLIC PERIOD

I. The Synoptic records preserve for us the teaching of Jesus almost exclusively in Galilee, to the husbandmen and fishermen of that province. They also give some account of controversies in Galilee with scribes and Pharisees, and in Jerusalem at the last feast. The Fourth Gospel on the other hand presents a different kind of utterance. Controversy about His person and work fills a large place in its records. In the latter half there is the report of teachings of a much more advanced kind which could not have been understood by the multitudes. Without entering into the difficult critical questions* involved, we may observe that if Jesus did teach at all after the manner shown in the Fourth Gospel, we have here a striking instance of His adaptation of Himself to His hearers. But even without taking into account the records of the Fourth Gospel, the Synoptic teaching proves how close Jesus could keep to His hearers. It was eternal truth that He was teaching, showing an unerring insight into the deep things of God as well as the heart of man, and yet He uses the speech of everyday life; the common things of the world around Him are made transparent symbols of the highest moral and spiritual reality. He had a keen eye to observe, and a quick heart to appreciate the ways and the works of men, and the familiar human relations and occupations became for His hearers the interpreters of the Kingdom. He recognized, sympathized with, and ministered to the common

* I have dealt with these problems in my book *The Beloved Disciple*.

needs of men. Unfettered by, He attached Himself to the teaching of the Old Testament; the spiritual inheritance of His people was taken up into the treasure of the soul that He Himself bestowed on men. All that had essential significance and permanent value in the Old revelation was preserved in the New. In this respect Jesus Himself is an example to the Christian preacher.

II. Owing to the reserve in speech and restraint in action He exercised, the contrast between His message and the contemporary Judaism did not become so manifest as it was when the confession of His Messiahship and the proclamation of His saving death and triumphant resurrection by His apostles disclosed the breach between Christian faith and Jewish belief.

(1) It is true that the apostles in the Church at Jerusalem remained Jews, and were not fully conscious that they were called to be the agents of a new moral and religious creation. Nevertheless these facts of which they were the witnesses, and the faith which was based upon these facts separated them by a widening gulf from their fellow countrymen. The wider Hellenistic culture of Stephen made him aware of the change as the apostles themselves were not. Even although the Master Himself had failed to win the people, the disciples dared to believe that they could achieve what He had failed in doing. Undoubtedly for a time and in a measure, filled with the zeal and power of Pentecost, they did succeed in winning a multitude to accept their testimony and yield to their influence although, as

after-events showed, the conversion from the old beliefs to the new faith was in many instances far less thorough than at first appeared. The Jerusalem Church remained, to a large extent, Judaist and Judaizing.

(2) In the days of the earthly ministry the disciples were often slow of heart to believe, because dull of mind to understand, their Master's teaching; even after Pentecost they learned very slowly; they clung to the familiar shores of Judaism instead of launching out into the deep of their world-wide mission. The forty days which elapsed between the Passover and Pentecost show how slowly the conviction that Jesus had risen, and lived, and reigned, took full possession, becoming a certainty which could inspire confidence and courage. Peter's speeches in Acts * do give indications that the meaning of the death of Christ in the light of the Resurrection only slowly disclosed itself. How distrustful the primitive community remained of any extension of its mission beyond the Jewish people, the records about Samaria (Acts viii, 14-17), and Antioch show (xi, 19-23), and even of Peter's reception after his return from the home of Cornelius (xi. 1-4). Unwilling to go out to the Gentiles, the Jerusalem Church failed to prevent the tragedy of the fall of the city, resulting from Jewish fanaticism. The insignificance of Jewish Christianity after this event shows that the organism of the primitive Church had not reacted potently enough on its environment to preserve its own life and to trans-

* Compare Acts ii. 14-36 ; iii. 12-26 ; v. 29-32.

form its surroundings. The new life had to make a new body for itself in the Gentile Churches founded by Paul. We have here an example of a religious conservatism that should serve as a warning against acquiescence in conditions which need to be changed, if progress is to be secured.

(3) This is not, however, all that we may learn from the Church in Jerusalem. Peter did endeavour in his preaching to fulfil his Master's injunction to be a scribe who has been made a disciple of the Kingdom, and brings forth out of his treasure things new and old (Matthew xiii, 52). He did proclaim the human crime of the Cross, and the divine vindication of the Resurrection, and because of that vindication he could find in the crime even a divine necessity, the fulfilment of prophecy. This was the primitive apologetic*: " that Christ died for our sins according to the Scriptures; and that He was buried; and that He has been raised on the third day according to the Scriptures " (1 Cor. xv. 3, 4). This was the common testimony. The facts were authenticated by eye-witnesses; and their significance was interpreted by means of the Scriptures. In the circumstances no more persuasive or convincing method could have been used. This was the argument and appeal to the outside world; within the Church, as the preservation of the teaching of Jesus in the Synoptic Gospels shows, fuller instruction was given in the life and

---

* In numerous articles Dr. J. Rendel Harris has shown how important and general in the Church from the earliest days was this use of the Old Testament.

teaching of Jesus. It may be that this was the distinctive function of the ministers, called evangelists or teachers, who rank next to apostles and prophets. The apostles were primarily witnesses of the facts and their meanings, the prophets were men who in an exalted state of feeling, uttered the will of God as disclosed to them. What is significant for our present purpose is the adjustment to the environment in the use of the argument from prophecy; it was not an artificial adjustment, but a natural, for the faith of the preachers themselves was confirmed by the means which they employed to commend their testimony to others. Here were the points of contact between preachers as Christian believers and hearers as pious Jews; and the most and best uses were made of this avenue of approach.

(4) Although presented to us as Epistles, yet Hebrews and James may be regarded as homilies, as instances of preaching, belonging according to many scholars to the latter half of the first century. These two Epistles form a very striking contrast. In James the Christian element is not absent, but much which is distinctive of it is lacking: the Jewish element survives in a very dominant note. It shows how much of a Jew a Christian believer might remain. Whether the apostle James, the head of the Church in Jerusalem, wrote it or not, the Epistle shows us what kind of Christian instruction made it possible for many thousands among the Jews to believe, and yet remain zealous for the law (Acts xxi. 20). A remarkable feature of the Epistle

ience through which he passed—destructive of the old and creative of the new—secured that he never would lose his own self as Christ was making him, but would only the more potently exercise the influence of that self, and the Christ in him to save the men whom he so approached. Paul, the essential Paul, Christ's new creation, was preserved in all his adjustments of his mission and message to the world in which he laboured.

(b) While we cannot take the records in Acts of Paul's preaching as *verbatim* reports, yet we are justified in assuming that they represent the substance of what he said on each occasion. They prove how skilfully he adapted his utterance to his hearers. His speech at Lystra (Acts xiv. 15-17) is an appeal, such as his rustic hearers, interested in seasons and harvests, could appreciate. His speech at Athens (Acts xvii. 22-31) cannot be regarded as a mistake, afterwards confessed in 1 Cor. ii. 1-2 as such, as some have rather presumptuously maintained, but was adapted to get him a hearing, as another mode of approach would not have been. He was not omitting the Gospel, but preparing the way for it as verse 31 shows. Would his hearers have listened to him at all, had he begun with " Jesus Christ and Him crucified " ? That the levity of his hearers frustrated his attempt does not prove the futility of his endeavour on this as on other occasions to be " all things to all men that he might save some." How suitable to the occasion are the two speeches delivered in the synagogue at Antioch of Pisidia (xiii. 16-41, 46-47). How far the eschatological teaching of 1 Thessalonians afterwards guarded against misconception in 2 Thess., represented his ordinary teaching in Christian congregations is uncertain. What is certain from 1 Cor. xv. 3-4 is that the Crucifixion and the Resurrection and their interpretation in the light of the Old Testament Scriptures had a large place in the Christian message he delivered in all the Churches.

(c) As the founder of Churches he moved from place to place, and his letters take the place to a large extent of the ministry of preaching of the pastor of to-day. We are entitled then to use these letters to illustrate what manner of preacher Paul was. When we compare *Galatians* and *Romans* on the one hand with *Ephesians* and *Colossians* on the other, we discover how fully he could be a Jew to Jews, and a Greek to Greeks. When he is seeking to justify his Gospel against Judaizers he can use the terms familiar to Pharisaic Judaism. When he is endeavouring to maintain the supremacy of Christ as Saviour and Lord against Gentile heretical speculations, he can make his own the phraseology current in those circles. While we must not regard his treatment of the work of Christ or the person of Christ as merely an accommodation to those with whom he was dealing, as for himself the exposition he gave was significant and valuable; yet we are justified in distinguishing such an apologetic treatment of any matter from the dogmatic confession of what was most distinctive in his own personal experience. We feel ourselves nearer the heart of Paul in Gal. ii, 19-21, than in verses 15-18, and in Romans vi. 1-11 than in iii. 21-31.

(d) What has been called his *faith-mysticism*, his personal union with Christ by faith in His grace, is more the essential Paul than his forensic doctrine of the Atonement, or his metaphysical doctrine of the divinity of Christ. He could afford to be a Jew to Jews and a Greek to Greeks, because there was a vigorous personality with a vital experience to save accommodation from becoming compromise, and to give a distinct and constant Christian content to every presentation—Jewish or Greek—of his message. While the Christian preacher must avoid any such protrusion of himself in his preaching as can be charged with egotism, yet Paul does show that the personality, experience and character of the preacher must, and ought to come to expression in his preaching. The preaching that is impersonal, the transmission of a creed, and not the confession of a life has less interest and effect than that in which the truth comes through the personality. Autobiographical a preacher need not be, as Paul often necessarily was, since he represents a historical community of faith. But his witness will have effect as he is himself presenting that witness in words that live because he himself is living in them the life which Christ lives in him. That to some preachers may sound too mystical but that is the secret of the preaching of Paul, and well it is for any preacher who can share that secret of the " life hid with Christ in God."

(2) It is not necessary to discuss any of the

critical questions raised by the Fourth Gospel, and the Epistles dependent on it.

(a) In the Prologue we have an instance of becoming a Greek to the Greeks. Whatever be the source of the contents of the Prologue, whether Palestinian in the Wisdom literature, or Hellenistic in the philosophy of Philo, it is placed at the beginning of the Gospel to commend that Gospel to the thinkers of the Gentile environment, in which the Gospel was composed. It would in my judgment, however, be a mistake to assume that the character of the record itself has been affected by the metaphysics of the Prologue. There are passages in the Gospel which show the same metaphysical interest; but for the most part what we can trace in the Gospel is another process, the transformation of reminiscence by reflexion; whether these reflexions came from the same person as the reminiscences is not absolutely certain, but they are generally so closely blended that it is probable that the same disciple of Jesus—whoever he may have been— under what he believed to be the illumination of the Spirit of God let his memories pass through his meditations.

(b) A generation at least must have elapsed between the events and the comments, and this lapse of time represented an inward development, in which there was a recovery of the past that was a continuous transformation of it. We can notice the change which reflexion wrought in reminiscence in three respects: the historical personality remembered is changed into the eternal presence experienced, the outward discipleship becomes a constant inward communion, and consequently the eschatology of the Second Advent, the General Resurrection and the Final Judgment, is replaced by the present rising from the death in unbelief to the life in faith, the present possession of the eternal life, and the present judgment of salvation for the believer, and condemnation for all who do not believe. If even reminiscences were so altered by reflexion in a living mind, because of the inspiration of the Spirit of God, should not the Christian preacher welcome in himself a continuous development in his thought of the truth he preaches ? As in the Johannine writings the development was not a purely subjective process, unrelated to the environment, but, because related, a condition of the adaptation of the Gospel to the changing world, so as the preacher grows with his surroundings can he have a living message for his age. In the Johannine writings we can trace a more marked development as covering a longer period of time than we can in Paul, although Paul's theology also shows some signs of change. Consequently in the Johannine writings there seems to be less conscious adaptation to the environment than in Paul. The evangelist did not with such deliberate intent need to become a Greek to the Greeks as did Paul, but a long life allowed the Jew in him to recede more and more, and to give place to the Greek. In both cases there is both inward development and outward adaptation, but the proportions are not exactly the same.

(3) Again and again has the Christian Church

been less effective in its task because there has been too rigid an adherence to the traditions of the past, too facile a refusal to understand the needs of the world. The message that the age would have been ready to accept has been refused, and outworn ideas and terms been emphasized. "Of the translation of the problem of the Incarnation into Greek in the subsequent centuries," Dr. Cave writes (and his words enforce the lesson the Apostolic Age has for the Christian preacher), "such a translation was necessary if Christianity was to become more than a Jewish sect. It brought with it many perils; it led to inadequate views of Christ, and to subversions of Christianity more dangerous than any that could have come from Jewish thought. But it put Christianity into relation with contemporary culture, made it appear as a native and not an exotic, religion, and made possible its statement in categories through which alone it could become intelligible and attractive to the non-Jewish world. The treasure of the Gospel is always in an earthen vessel, and in the Greek world this earthen vessel was now to be of Greek, and not Jewish manufacture." As Dr. Cave was a missionary in India for some years, a footnote he adds has great value. "Here, too, an illustration from the modern mission field may be permissible. The early Protestant missionaries in India rigidly opposed any attempt to interpret Christianity in terms of Hindu thought. In consequence Christianity remained orthodox (by Western standards) but foreign and unintelligible. If like the evangelists they had ventured to impress into the service of Christ a pagan term, and spoken of the Incarnation as an *avatāra*, doubtless there would have been Indian heresies, but by now the Indian Church would probably be less alien and exotic, and better able to formulate its own theology. It is not in biology alone that life means response to environment." * This adjustment has its dangers, lest the treasure be hidden in, or soiled by, the earthen vessel. But there are two safeguards, a personal experience of union with Christ, and consequent conformity to His death and His life, such as Paul had, who could say of himself with truth: " To me to live is Christ " (Phil. i. 21), and a personal development under the illumination of the Spirit of God as the author of the Fourth Gospel indirectly claims for himself in the words he ascribes to Christ, " When He the Spirit of truth, is come, He shall guide you into all the truth " (John xvi, 13).

* *The Doctrine of the Person of Christ*, pp. 67-68.

CHAPTER III

THE PATRISTIC PERIOD

As has been shown already in the preceding chapter the organism of the Christian Church began to adapt itself to the Gentile environment within the Apostolic Age. This process was carried further in the subsequent period, called the Patristic, because its teachers were regarded as having laid down the doctrines and practices which should be authoritative for all coming generations. This process of adaptation was inevitable; but in the judgment of reformers of later centuries it was carried further than even the times demanded, and resulted in making the Church less Christian and more pagan than the necessary self-development in the new situation required. In this environment the two potent factors were Greek culture and Roman law and order. The doctrine of the Church was cast into the moulds of Greek thought; and, although the antithesis which Dr. Hatch presents between the Sermon on the Mount and the Nicene Creed* goes beyond the facts, as the teaching of Jesus Himself was not confined to the contents of the Sermon on the Mount; and although the term *secularization* which Harnack† uses is an exaggera-

* *The Hibbert Lectures,* 1888, p. 1.
† *History of Dogma,* II, p. 18.

tion, nevertheless the truth of the Gospel was forced into philosophical terminology alien to its characteristics. As dominant on the organization of the Church was the Roman influence. The Papacy with its pretensions to temporal power is the heir of the Cæsars. Into the worship of the Church many pagan superstitions and corruptions were allowed to intrude. In many respects the Christian Church won that Graeco-Roman world by losing its own distinctive soul. In defending itself against what it was conscious of being hostile to itself—persecution, and heresy or schism—in adapting itself with less consciousness of what was involved to what in the environment it could assimilate, the Christian Church believed itself to be preserving continuity with the past, the Apostolic Age, in three ways. "Three standards," says Harnack, "are to be kept in view, viz., the apostolic doctrine, the apostolic canon of Scripture, and the guarantee of apostolic authority, afforded by the organization of the Church, that is, by the episcopate, and traced back to apostolic institution. . . . They originated in Rome and gradually made their way in the other Churches." * What the fathers sought to do was to formulate the theology of the Church in accordance with these standards. Whether these standards were really as apostolic as they were believed to be, and whether the fathers succeeded in maintaining as complete an accord with these standards as they themselves desired are questions the answer to which lies beyond the purpose of

* *Op. cit.*, p. 19.

this volume; so much it has been necessary to state to provide the historical background for the preachers of whom some account will be given.* In selecting three for notice, Origen, Chrysostom, and Augustine I have been guided by the personal interest that attaches to them and their value as historical illustrations of the preacher's functions.

I. While on account of what was afterwards deemed to be the heretical character of some of his doctrines, Origen has not been called saint, and his claim to be reckoned one of the fathers would be challenged; yet as regards his personality he was much more nearly conformed to the apostolic standard of saint than many who have borne that title.

(1) Of his education Eusebius gives us a most charming account. In a time of persecution " such desire for martyrdom seized the soul of Origen, although yet a boy," that " his mother hid all his clothing, and thus compelled him to remain at home. But, as there was nothing else that he could do, and his zeal beyond his age would not suffer him to be quiet, he sent to his father an encouraging letter on martyrdom, in which he exhorted him, saying, ' Take heed not to change your mind on our account.' This may be recorded as the first evidence of Origen's youthful wisdom and of his genuine love of piety. For even then he had stored up no small resources in the words of the faith, having been trained in the Divine Scriptures from

* See *The Christian Preacher*. Part I. Chapter III.

childhood." Afterwards followed the study of
" the Greek sciences." While his father found it
necessary sometimes to rebuke his curiosity beyond
his years, concerning the meaning of the Scriptures,
" by himself he rejoiced greatly and thanked God,
the Author of all good, that He had deemed him
worthy to be the father of such a child. And they
say that often, standing by the boy when asleep,
he uncovered his breast, as if the Divine Spirit
were enshrined within it, and kissed it reverently;
considering himself blessed in his goodly off-
spring."*

(2) His Christian home, his early piety, his ardent
devotion, his manifold learning both in the Scriptures and in the culture of the age, and the inspiration of the example of his martyr father, combined
to make Origen from early manhood the kind of
personality through whom the truth of the Gospel
may be mediated. Supporting himself in his poverty
by giving instruction in the Greek literature of
which he had acquired a mastery, he boldly in a
time of persecution preached the Gospel, instructed
Gentiles who " came to him with a mind to hear
the word of God," associated himself so openly
with the martyrs, that he was near becoming a victim
of the violence of the pagan mob. At the age of
eighteen he was appointed head of the catechetical
school of Alexandria. When the demands of this
school upon him increased he abandoned his former
sole means of livelihood, and declining any fees,

* *The Church History of Eusebius*, VI, 2. (McGiffert's Translation, p. 250.)

he secured a pittance for his own support by selling
his manuscripts of the Greek classics which he
possessed, many of which he had himself trans-
cribed, to a literary collector. " Even so he trembled
as he repeated the words: ' He that forsaketh not
all that he hath cannot be My disciple.' The very
existence of such a man was a tower of strength
to Christianity ; for of him it was literally
true, as Eusebius says, that ' he taught as he
lived, and lived as he taught.' "* Although he
almost courted martyrdom, yet " the celestial grace
as often protected him in danger." He carried his
asceticism to an extreme in his desire to realize
what he regarded as the Christian ideal. Taking
Matt. xix. 12 literally as an injunction of the Lord,
" he also rashly perpetrated an act of self-mutilation
which he afterwards regretted, and which was yet
adversely to influence his future." † His growing
fame as a teacher afterwards aroused the jealousy
of his bishop Demetrius; and he was driven from
Alexandria. " With such a record as he had behind
him, with his unequalled ability, and with such
powerful friends as the bishops who had ordained
him, Origen might have been the leader of a great
party, and fought Demetrius on equal terms, had
he so chosen. But he abhorred schism, and with
noble Christian unselfishness counted no sacrifice
too great in order to maintain the unity of Christ's
Church. Not waiting for any formal sentence of

* *Origen and Greek Patristic Theology*, by W. Fairweather pp.
41-42.
† Fairweather, *op. cit.*, p. 43.

deprivation, he quietly took leave of the place that was dearer to him than any other on earth, never, as it chanced, to set foot in it again. 'Great even from his cradle,' as Jerome says, Origen never showed himself greater than at this critical juncture in his career." * For the rest of his life, till his death in 253 or 254, he was a wanderer, preaching, teaching, and suffering persecution.

(3) In his teaching he strove for a reconciliation of Christian truth and Greek philosophy. While there is no ground for the assumption that at the age of thirty he underwent a sudden conversion to Platonism, there is good reason to believe that he did resume his studies of Greek literature in order to qualify himself the better as a Christian apologist. He himself states: " When I had devoted myself entirely to theology, and the fame of my skill in that department began to be noised abroad, and sometimes heretics, sometimes those who had studied the Greek sciences, and philosophy in particular, came to visit me, I deemed it advisable to investigate both the doctrinal views of the heretics and what the philosophers claimed to know of the truth."† Without going into any details of his teaching, two features of it may be mentioned. He expounded the Scriptures by the method of allegorizing, for which he found both a Scriptural and a Platonic basis. In Proverbs xxii. 20: " Have not I written unto thee excellent things," of the word *excellent*, the R.V. marg. states in a note, " The word is

* Fairweather, *op. cit.*, pp. 51-52.
† Fairweather, *op. cit.*, pp. 43-44.

doubtful." The Septuagint and the Vulgate render the word "thrice" or in triple form (τρισσῶς tripliciter). According to Plato man consists of body, soul, and spirit; so in the Scriptures there is a *somatic* (literal or historical) meaning, a *psychic* (doctrinal and practical) and a *pneumatic* (mystical or speculative). By this method of interpretation under the influence of Greek philosophy he was led to doctrinal conclusions, which were not in accord with the common creed. He was thus forced to make a distinction between faith (πίστις) and knowledge (γνῶσις), the exoteric doctrine for the common Christian believer, and the esoteric for the instructed Christian theologian. Dangerous as this distinction may sometimes prove to be " it was just because of this that he was so successful as a Christian missionary to the Greeks. It would be wrong to say that he proclaimed two Christianities; what he really asserted was that one Christian saw much more in Christianity than another."* What Origen teaches the preacher for to-day is that he must expound the Scriptures by the best method available (which now is not the allegorical, but the historical); and that he, without neglecting the ordinary congregation, must seek to make Christianity intelligible to the cultured of the age.

II. " John, to whom an admiring posterity, since the seventh century, has given the name Chrysostomus, the Golden-mouthed, is the greatest expositor and preacher of the Greek Church, and still enjoys

* Fairweather, *op. cit.*, p. 90.

the highest honour in the whole Christian world. No one of the Oriental fathers has left a more spotless reputation, no one is so much read and so often quoted by modern commentators."*

(1) Of his mother Anthusa, left a widow from her twentieth year, Libanius, the famous pagan rhetorician, said: "Ah, what wonderful women there are among the Christians." Giving him the liberal education of the time, by her personal training she so implanted Christian faith in him from his earliest years that he was not allured by paganism. Libanius, to whom he owed his literary training, would have wished him for his successor "if only the Christians had not carried him away." For a short time he followed the career of a rhetorician, but soon decided to devote himself to Christian service. His mother's entreaties alone restrained him from the monastic life for a time, and he became a reader, but succeeded in evading election as a bishop. After his mother's death he left the city for six years of quiet and study in a monastery near Antioch. By excessive self-mortification, for he was as extreme an ascetic as Origen, he injured his health; and returning to Antioch as a preacher, both by his eloquence and his character he acquired a great reputation. After sixteen or seventeen years as a preacher he was chosen, without taking any action to this end himself, patriarch of Constantinople. (A.D. 397). He was unsparing in his condemnation of the luxury and the vice of his own

* *History of the Church,* by Schaff. *Nicene and Post-Nicene Christianity,* II, pp. 933-934.

age and surroundings; and he thus provoked the hostility of the empress Eudoxia, whom he dared to compare to Herodias thirsting for the blood of John. There had always been a rivalry between the Churches of Alexandria and of Constantinople; and their patriarchs had often been at variance. The ambitious patriarch, Theophilus of Alexandria, was filled with envy of the fame of Chrysostom, and conspired with Eudoxia against him. His kindness to persecuted Origenist monks involved him in the Origenistic controversy, and afforded his enemies the pretext for hostile action. Although the people was with him, and also Innocent of Rome, they prevailed; and he was driven into exile, where he died in 407.

(2) Despite his position as Patriarch of Constantinople he escaped its dangers, pride and worldliness; he lived as a poor man, and gave away most of the wealth that came to him to the poor. His eloquence often called forth the applause of his hearers; a passage in one of his sermons in which he condemned this abuse was itself applauded. While he had trained his natural gift in the rhetorical schools, his eloquence drew from a deeper fountain of inspiration, even an experience and a character in which the effectual working of the Holy Spirit was manifest. He was a diligent student of the Bible, and made careful preparation for preaching. But he sometimes soared highest in utterance when borne up on the wings of an inspiring occasion. He gave systematic expositions of whole books of the Bible, and was not content with the treatment

of isolated texts, as was the growing custom. While his language has many excellencies, there are in it at times artificialities and exaggerations which the current rhetorical methods commended, but which now offend our taste. He was copious rather than orderly, and sometimes erred by lack of reserve and restraint. He could deal with the depths of " the inner life," as he had fathomed these in his own experience, although he failed fully to understand Paul's doctrine of grace. He was at home in the Scriptures as a scholar, and could bring out of their store " treasures new and old." His vivid imagination and æsthetic sense enabled him to make persons and scenes from the Scriptures vitally real to his hearers. He displayed special skill in applying the teaching of the Scriptures to the practical affairs of men and even to public policy; and this he often did, as has already been indicated, at great risk to himself. But personal prudence did not hold him back from declaring " the whole counsel of God," as it was given to him to understand it.

(3) Himself a rigid ascetic, with a preference for the monastic life, of which he gives us a very bright picture, he condemned the extravagance and luxury that had become a morbid passion among many of his hearers, the aristocracy of the later Empire. He insisted on the exclusion of all unworthy persons from the communion. " Though a captain," says he to those who administer the communion, " or a governor, nay even one adorned with the imperial crown, approach (the table of the Lord)

unworthily, prevent him; you have greater authority than he. . . . Beware lest you excite the Lord to wrath and give a sword instead of food. And if a new Judas should appear, prevent him. Fear God, not man. If you fear man, he will treat you with scorn; if you fear God, you will appear venerable even to men." * High as he rose in his Christian character above his surroundings, he did not altogether escape the defects of his age. While commending Christian love even towards heretics and heathen, and opposed to the death penalty, he approved " the prohibition of their assemblies, and the confiscation of their churches." Elsewhere, however, he stated the worthier principle, that he himself would rather suffer than inflict injury. The most serious blot upon his character is one which offends us even in the theological expositions of the Greek fathers, a lack of veracity and honesty. He evaded election as a bishop, and thrust the office on his friend Basil by a ruse, which he thus justified: " Manifold is the potency of deception, only it must not be employed with knavish intent. And this should hardly be called deception, but rather a sort of accommodation (ὀικονομία) wisdom, art, or sagacity, by which one may find many ways of escape in an exigency, and amend the errors of the soul."† Courageous as he was, this confession shows that the Church of his own time had not emerged into the Christian sense of truthfulness, but was still submerged under the pagan sophistry, which

* Quoted by Schaff, *op. cit.*, I, pp. 358-359.
† *Idem,* p. 254.

even Plato defended. Apart from these defects, Chrysostom may be ranked among the greatest of Christian preachers, not golden-mouthed only, but golden-hearted.

III. Turning from the East to the West, there is one of the fathers, who is as was Saul among the people.

(1) So far as we can ascribe historical movements to any one personality, it was Augustine who made the difference between the Eastern and the Western Church. His recovery of the Pauline doctrines of grace gave to the Roman Church a religious vitality and moral vigour which the orthodoxy of the Greek Church failed to secure. " Between St. Paul the Apostle and Luther the Reformer, the Christian Church has possessed no one who could measure himself with Augustine; and in comprehensive influence no other is to be compared with him. We are right, both in the Middle Ages and to-day, to mark a distinction between the spirit of the East and that of the West; and we are right to observe in the latter a life and motion, the straining of mighty forces, high problems, and great aims. But if so, the *Church* of the West at least owes this peculiarity of hers in no small degree to one man, Augustine. Along with the Church he served, he has moved through the centuries. We find him in the great mediæval theologians, including the greatest, Thomas Aquinas. His spirit sways the pietists and mystics of those ages; St. Bernard no less than Thomas à Kempis. It is he that inspires the ecclesiastical reformers—those of the Karling epoch as much as

a Wyclif, a Huss, a Wesel, and a Wessel; while on the other hand it is the same man that gives to the ambitious popes the ideal of a theocratic state to be realized on earth."*

(2) In Augustine a Pauline believer, a Platonist philosopher, and a Roman churchman were blended in the unity of a spiritual genius of the first order. His personality is familiar to us as few others can be, for in his Confessions he has himself laid bare his inner life to us. " The significance of the ' Confessions ' is as great on the side of form as on that of content. Before all, they were a literary *achievement*. No poet, no philosopher before him undertook what he here performed. . . . What do the ' Confessions ' of Augustine contain ? The portrait of a soul—not psychological disquisitions on the Understanding, the Will, and the Emotions in Man, not abstract investigations into the nature of the soul, not superficial reasonings and moralizing introspections like the Meditations of Marcus Aurelius, but the most exact portraiture of a distinct human personality, in his development from childhood to full age, with all his propensities, feelings, aims, mistakes; a portrait of a soul in fact, drawn with a perfection of observation that leaves on one side the mechanical devices of psychology, and pursues the method of the physician and the physiologist "† Augustine was forty-four years of age when he wrote this marvellous record of the dealings of God with him.

* Harnack. *Confessions of St. Augustine*, pp. 123-124.
† Harnack, *op. cit.*, pp. 127-128.

(3) Unlike Origen and Chrysostom he was not born as a child into the Kingdom of God; but the solicitude of his Christian mother Monica and her prayers found their fulfilment in his conversion only when he was thirty-three. Throughout the years of his enslavement to the lusts of the flesh, and the wanderings of his intellect in the Manichæan heresy, academic scepticism and Platonic idealism, he maintained his keenness of intellect, his sensitiveness of conscience, his religious aspirations. He describes his conversion in the Confessions, Book VIII, Chapter XII. Obeying the " voice, as of a boy or girl," repeating the words, " Take read, take read," he read the words in Romans xiii. 13, 14, " No further would I read; nor was there need; for instantly at the end of this sentence, as though my heart were flooded with a light of peace, all the shadows of doubt melted away." It was his experience that made his theology; he taught the bondage of the human will, and the power of the divine grace because he had experienced the one and the other. Other elements were mingled in his thinking, but it was this experience of salvation from sin by the grace of God which was its distinctive feature. Baptized in 387 by Ambrose, he abandoned the world, and devoted himself entirely to the service of God.

(4) Four years later he was, against his will, chosen presbyter by the voice of the people; and after four years again elected Bishop of Hippo Regius in Africa; and there for thirty-eight years he laboured till his death. He lived as an ascetic,

but did not carry his asceticism to the extreme. Often he preached five days in succession and sometimes twice in one day. His one theme was the Gospel of salvation. Of his manifold activities as theologian, controversialist, and ecclesiastic it is not necessary here to speak, but only of his eminence as a preacher. Although he was inferior to Chrysostom as an orator he was a greater personality with a deeper experience of saving grace. He was less of a scholar too, but by the use of the allegorical method he could draw the Gospel richly out of the Old as well as the New Testament. One special gift he had was that of saying *multum in parvo*. He expressed a truth in the fewest words possible, and yet so strikingly that the saying could not be forgotten. Many of these sayings have become the current coin of the Christian pulpit.

(5) We are fortunate in having in the fourth book of his *De Doctrina Christiana* his own homiletics. Pulpit eloquence is distinguished from the rhetoric of the schools by the possession of a wisdom from above which can see with " the eyes of the heart the heart of the Scriptures." In agreement with Cicero he describes the orator's task as to teach, to please, and to move, to enlighten the mind, win the heart, and bend the will. There are three manners, the lowly, the lofty, and the middle mode of speech. The content must determine what the manner shall be; and nevertheless to avoid monotony there should be as much variety of manner as the subject will allow. In accordance with his themes, the great verities of the Gospel, he himself excelled in the

grand style; but he did not disdain simple, striking imagery, antitheses and epigrams, and other rhetorical devices to sustain interest by variety of presentation. It may appear strange that this brief account of Augustine, which began with an indication of his historical greatness, should end in this description of his theory of preaching in what might seem insignificant details. And yet there is no incongruity. The style is the man; that does not mean that the great man can be careless of his style, trusting to his greatness to make his style great. It is true that if a man intensely desires to say something, it is probable that he will get it said effectively, as emotion quickens imagination and intellect. And yet it will not be said so perfectly, if he has not disciplined himself, so that art has become his second nature and his spontaneous utterance becomes aesthetically satisfying. The preacher should, as did Augustine, study how to say best what is the best for him to say.*

---

* I have not discussed in this volume the subject of *Homiletics*, the theory and art of preaching, but may refer the readers to *A Guide to Preachers*, Third Section, dealing with *How to Preach* ; also, *The Christian Preacher*, Part III, discussing *the Preparation and the Production of a Sermon.*

CHAPTER IV

THE SCHOLASTIC PERIOD

DURING the Patristic Period the Christian Church adapted itself to its environment in the Graeco-Roman world. After the fall of the Western Empire, and the incursion of the barbarian peoples, which were in course of time to develop into the nations of Modern Europe, it had an enlarged and altered environment. It came too late in the history of the Roman Empire to preserve it, but it did conserve the culture of that ancient world for the modern. It was the means of subjugating barbarism to Christian religion and morals, although in this process the environment reacted on the organism as in the previous period. The new peoples brought their contribution of fresh life to the progress of the world, and in the Renaissance and Reformation they sought emancipation from the subjection to the Church of Rome which had been a necessary condition of their own development. In this transmission and diffusion of the inheritance of the past by the Church preaching had a large part.* Interesting as is the story of the missionary activity of the Church of which for the most part monks were the agents, it must here be passed over; a full

* See *The Christian Preacher*, Part I, Chapter IV.

79

account of it may be found in C. H. Robinson's *The Conversion of Europe*. In the previous period most of the preaching was done by the bishop; but as the diocese grew larger, that ministry had largely to be delegated to the priest of the parish. Despite efforts to assist the clergy in the discharge of their duty, there was a steady decline of preaching between A.D. 800 and 1200, when a recovery took place.

I. The Crusades exercised a very marked influence on thought and life. Religious zeal was quickened; the peoples were brought into closer contact with one another in their common enterprise. In directing the Christian imagination to the sacred places of the Gospel story the Crusades helped to restore the Jesus of history to the Christian heart. There was even a revival of learning owing to contact with the Saracens, who in their science and philosophy were in advance of Christendom. Through this channel Aristotle came to be better known, and the development of scholasticism was stimulated. Scholasticism may be briefly described as the attempt to make intelligible by means of the Aristotelian philosophy, as it was then known and understood, the ecclesiastical dogma of the Church. Anselm's phrase *credo ut intelligam*, I believe that I may understand, is the clue to scholasticism. The authority of the Church was primary, and reason could be used only to demonstrate the truth of that teaching. But along with scholasticism, and often in alliance with it, there was another movement—that of mysticism. Through the writings of the Pseudo-

Dionysius, translated from Greek into Latin by
John Scotus Erigena, the Neo-Platonic mysticism
found a home within the Christian Church; but in
its leading representatives in the Middle Ages it
assumed the form of a loving communion with
Christ as the Bridegroom of the soul. All these
currents meet in the life and work of Bernard of
Clairvaux (died 1153) who was the greatest preacher
of the twelfth century. Bernard was a great theologian exercising a very powerful influence. He
was the most formidable opponent of Abelard,
who put forward what is generally described as
the subjective or moral theory of the Atonement,
namely, that Christ's death was an appeal of the
love of God in suffering to move man to penitence
and faith. He was opposed to the method of
Abelard as unduly exalting the human understanding in dealing with the divine mysteries.
While he did not depreciate learning, he insisted
on its subordination to piety.

(a) His own piety was intensely mystical, and
found its appropriate and congenial expression in
the language of the Song of Songs; his passionate
devotion to Jesus appropriated the endearments
of sexual passion. His sermons on the *Song of
Songs* were delivered to the monks of his own order
that they might share his own intense mysticism.
What he longed and hoped for was that he might
be allowed to kiss the heavenly bridegroom on his
lips. This analogy, however, carries with it the
peril of familiarity and irreverence; it imports a
sensuousness into the relation, from which even

Bernard did not altogether escape, and which assumed much more offensive form in other mystics, especially women. A welcome feature of this mysticism, however, is the stress Bernard puts on the self-humiliation of the Saviour, His lowliness and suffering. He in this way recovered in some measure the Pauline type of piety with its insistence on divine grace and human faith ; he anticipated Luther's teaching on justification by faith. Addressing Christ in a sermon he says, after giving instances from the earthly ministry: " Thou art as able to justify, as abounding to forgive. Wherefore whosoever, contrite for his sins, hungers and thirsts for righteousness, believes in Thee, who dost justify the ungodly, he also justified by faith alone will have peace with God." Although his mysticism brought him into so intimate communion with Christ in His grace, yet inconsistently he asserts the mediation of the mother of Jesus in language that goes beyond any that Augustine had used. The mysticism of Bernard did not set aside the ordinances of the Church; the sacraments of the Church must be used, but taken up into the inner life, in which the soul is purified, illumined, and unified with God (*unformed, informed, transformed*). In the purification, for instance, the Confessional must be used, and the whole sacrament of penitence. Thus Bernard's piety did not modify his churchmanship.

(*b*) As Abbot of the Cistercian monastery of Clairvaux from A.D. 1115 he gave that order the highest place among all others in the esteem of his age; and by his personal friendship with Peter the Venerable he reconciled it with the Benedictine order of the monastery of Clugny. In his honour the French Cistercians assumed the name of Bernardines. Even the popes were ready to receive his counsel and admonition. In France, Italy, and Germany Bernard by his preaching summoned princes and peoples to take part in the Second Crusade in 1146. As the fall of Edessa threatened the safety of the Christian Kingdom, founded in 1099 in Jerusalem as a result of the First Crusade, the Pope Eugenius III had again called the nations to arms. Louis VII of France responded to the summons; and Bernard by his preaching so moved Conrad III of Germany, that with hesitation he followed the example. Bernard confidently predicted victory; but the attempt proved a pitiable failure. The language Bernard used in advocating the Crusade shows the spirit of the Old Testament at the time of the Judges rather than of the New. It is, and must remain a puzzle how one who could so appreciate the lowliness, tenderness, and gentleness of Christ should find it possible thus to declare the God of battles.

II. The supremacy of the Papacy which Innocent asserted at the Fourth Lateran Council in 1215, and for which Hildebrand had striven, was obtained by the sacrifice of religion

(a) The Church, at this moment, however, secured an auxiliary which was effective both in the revival of religion and in the support of the papal claims. Innocent encouraged the mendicants or friars in their efforts to teach the people the Bible and the truths of Christianity; and subsequent popes knew how to use them for their worldly ends as a counter-weight to any opposition of the national clergy. Dominic by his own preaching and the order he founded aimed at the rooting-out of all heresy. Although the Dominicans (*Domini canes*, the Lord's hounds) acquired notoriety as zealous servants of the Inquisition, it is probable that Dominic himself took no part in any persecution but sought to recover the heretics only by the ministry of preaching. The two preachers of greatest fame and widest influence belonged to the Franciscan order, Antony of Padua (*c.* 1195-1231) and Berthold of Regensburg (*c.* 1220-1272). They preached in many lands to audiences that were said to number tens of thousands. In both of these orders attention was given to the theory as well as the practice of preaching. Although after a time the preaching of the two orders deteriorated, yet there can be no doubt that that preaching was the most potent factor in sustaining the religious and moral life of the people for several centuries; and the services rendered by the friars deserve grateful recognition.

(*b*) In this movement there stands out in bold relief one man as worthy of the highest possible admiration. If the title of saint is to be used of any man few deserve it as did Francis of Assisi (1182-1226).* The son of a prosperous cloth merchant,

* See the English Translation of Sabatier's *Vie de S. François d'Assisi* and Dobson's *The Little Poor Man of Assisi*.

and of a mother who probably was of a noble family of Provence, his baptismal name John was afterwards changed by his father to Francis, a change for which three reasons have been suggested, his father's love for France, or a compliment to his French mother, or the boy's facility in learning French, a language which as the speech of the Troubadours was dear to him. Having received the education then available only for the children of rich parents, he joined his father in business, but his wealth secured for him an entry among the sons of the nobles. He took the popular side in a contest between the people and the nobles. After a brief experience of war, he changed his manner of life, and resolved to make Poverty his bride; it was with due deliberation that he gave effect to this resolve to be a mendicant. He devoted himself to the care of the lepers. According to one legend the crisis of his religious conversion was reached when he was praying before a crucifix in the poor Church of St. Damian. The Crucified became alive, and spoke His acceptance of Francis' dedication of himself to service. Unhindered by his father's wrath, he abandoned all to obey the call of Christ, as did Gautama the Buddha, when he realized the pain and grief in the world. This renunciation was his emancipation; for he rejoiced in poverty as bringing him nearer to the estate of Jesus Christ. His second call to missionary work and the founding of an order came to him in 1209 in Portiuncula. " One day he heard the priest at Mass reading, but it was Christ who seemed to say that he should go and preach, healing the sick, cleansing the lepers, raising the dead, and casting out devils, and that he should provide neither gold, nor silver, nor brass, nor scrip, nor shoes, nor staves. This was the formal commission for Francis for his labour and his poverty; and when he received it he cast aside staff and shoes and began to preach, or rather to speak to the people words of religion. For two years he had been preparing for his mission by renunciation of the things of the world, and he who had left all to follow Christ had a right to ask others to go with him. Francis entered upon his mission not as a novice in piety, but as one having authority." *

(c) How the order grew need not here be recorded. Its labours were not confined to Christendom, but the Gospel was carried to Moslem lands. Francis himself failed to reach the East and Morocco, and it is uncertain whether he got to the Moors in Spain. The disappointment due to the action of the Papacy in seeking to use the movement in its own interests and the humiliation inflicted upon himself he endured in loyalty to the Church and in submission to the will of God. While devoted to poverty, he was not opposed to labour for daily bread, but he feared learning lest it might draw his friars away from the love of Christ. He himself to the end lived so Christ-like a life that men were ready to believe,when Brother Elias after his death, announced that the body bore " the stigmata of Christ, for his hands and feet bore marks as of nails without

* *Francis and Dominic*, by J. Herkless, p. 24.

and within, forming a sort of scars; while at the side he was as if pierced with a lance, and often a little blood oozed from it."* Setting aside the possibility of a miracle, the probability of a physiological explanation cannot be altogether excluded. But even if the whole story must be rejected as a " pious fraud," what remains true is that few believers have been in spirit and effort so truly crucified with Christ as was the lovable brother of man, beast, bird and flower.

III. Ecclesiastic as Bernard of Clairvaux was, yet his mysticism bore him into a region beyond the dogma and ritual of the Church, which he approved, but by which he did not really live. Francis of Assisi, obedient son of the Church, aimed and achieved a Christ-like life, the roots of which were in no external ordinances, but were " hid with Christ in God." But the desire for something truer and better than the Church could offer became more explicit in some men who can be regarded as forerunners of the Reformation.

(a) Probably the greatest of these was John Wyclif (between 1320 and 1330-1384), an ecclesiastical statesman, a learned theologian, a translator of the Scriptures, a preacher and the founder of an order of preachers, the " poor priests," who preaching throughout the length and breadth of England became so great a power as to fill even the prelates with fear of their influence. His influence through John Huss (1369-1415) reached Bohemia, where a widespread and enduring movement of reform

* J. Herkless, *op. cit*, p. 59.

was achieved, even after Huss himself had sealed his witness with his blood. The same reforming spirit was shown in France by John Gerson (1363-1429), the Chancellor of the University of Paris, who boldly assailed the evils in the Church, and preached the Gospel of grace. The most striking personality among these " heralds of the dawn " was Savonarola (1452-1498), and of him a fuller account may be given.

(*b*) The literary genius of George Eliot has made the name of Savonarola familiar in circles in which the facts of the history of the Church are little known; for he is the dominating personality in her novel *Romola*, and the account she gives of one of his sermons, though " not a translation, but a free representation of his preaching in its more impassioned moments," does convey a true impression of what the man was, and how he preached. Prof. P. Villari's *Life and Times of Savonarola* has been translated into English by his wife. His preaching was prophetic, even apocalyptic. He denounced the sins of his age, and announced the judgment of God. He summoned the people to amendment and reform, and for a time a city was under his spell, and was moved to do what he willed. And the tragic close, when, abandoned by his friends and beset by his foes, he found his release amid the flames, has only served to make more assured his place among the martyrs for God, truth and righteousness, who command the gratitude and the reverence of mankind.

(*c*) Born of a noble family at Ferrara, he was

educated in the learning of the times, but ascetic in his disposition, he withdrew in his twenty-second year from secular public life, and entered a Dominican monastery at Bologna. His first appearance in San Marco, Florence, in 1482, proved a disappointment, but his second appearance seven years later redeemed the first failure. His apocalyptic preaching commanded the populace, but he incurred the hostility of the aristrocratic adherents of the Medici; there is, however, reason to doubt the story of his refusal to grant absolution to the dying Lorenzo the Magnifico. Appointed first vicar-general of the Dominican order in Tuscany in 1493, in less than two years he had incurred the hostility of the Papacy, and was summoned to Rome to answer a charge of heresy; and when he did not appear, he was forbidden to preach. Involved in the political troubles of his city, through what may now appear to us imprudent words and deeds, but what to him appeared the Lord's commission to His prophet, he was less able to stand against the authority of the Church. Defying the decree of excommunication pronounced in 1497, he continued his work; but the people now turned against him, and he was put on his trial. Under torture, he made avowals which he afterwards withdrew. The first trial revealed so little ground for extreme action that a second trial was found necessary; and after delays, due to difficulties between the political and ecclesiastical power, his enemies compassed their end, and he was sentenced to death.

(d) His historical significance has been described

by Dr. McHardy.* " He was the first mind in Italy, if not in Europe, to turn to effective original use the fresh intellectual life which the Renaissance had awakened—the first mind, nurtured under Renaissance influences, that struck out on a distinctly independent line, and brought the forces set free by the Renaissance to bear on some bold effort, which should mark a new move forward towards a higher civilization and a larger good for society and the race. Many others gathered up the scholarship of the Renaissance; many developed the critical faculty which it fostered; many imitated the polished grace of the restored classical literature. But to vitalize the learning and the quickened energies which the Renaissance supplied by a lofty enthusiasm for righteousness, and then so to use them as to break away into a fresh path of endeavour, suited to the needs of the age, and opening up to larger achievement in the ages to come—that was Savonarola's distinction. Amid imitations, pedantries, dilettanteisms, and elaborate scholarly trifling, his soul burned as with a fire for the great spiritual interests of existence; and the flame touched other hearts and lives, and set them palpitating with new hopes, new and purer aspirations, to such an extent as to give a higher direction to the emancipated life and mental activity of his time, and to convert that life and activity into the upward-straining, progressive force which brought the modern world into being."

* *Savonarola*, p. 8.

CHAPTER V

THE REFORMATION PERIOD

GREAT as the changes in human history may appear to be, yet closer scrutiny shows how real the continuity is. As was shown in the last section of the previous chapter, there was a preparation, intellectual, moral, and spiritual for the Reformation. An authority that was needed and beneficent, when the Roman Church was bringing the barbarian peoples into subjection to Christian morals and religion, had become a tyranny, which was increasingly felt to be intolerable by a developed reason and conscience. A growing national consciousness rebelled against the imposition in the name of Christ of an alien rule. There were political and intellectual no less than moral and religious factors in the historical process of the Reformation. The recognition of this fact is not a depreciation of the value of the religious influence in history, only an appreciation of the vital relation there is, and must be, between religion and the other contents of the thought and life of mankind. Great events are not produced solely by great men, but the great capacity must be joined with the great opportunity. John Wyclif and John Huss were great men, as great it may be as Luther; but they were "born out of due time"; the "fulness of the time" for the full effect of their vision and their ardour had not come. The is a truth that the hero-worshipper is in danger of forgetting. No less a mistake is it, however, to represent history as an impersonal process. The capacity must be there to match the opportunity; the man must be able and ready to know when the tide in the affairs of men is at the flood, and to take it. While as our purpose requires, our attention will be directed to personality as the potent factor in history, we must never allow ourselves to forget the outward conditions and the inward spirit of the age which allows the personality to achieve.*

I. Among the reformers the foremost place must be assigned to Martin Luther (1483-1546).

(a) It was no observation and calculation of favourable conditions, no interpretation even of the signs of the times that enabled him to achieve what he did; a deep need had been met by a rich experience and that experience urged him to a great enterprise. Some like Augustine feel most keenly the need of deliverance from the bondage of sin; others desire most of all the assurance of forgiveness. This was what brought distress of soul upon Luther; the ordinances of the Church hindered, and did not help the access to his need of the grace of God; and he had to recover the Pauline doctrine of justification by faith before he found peace to his soul. That recovery was only gradually gained. "An aged monk asked him to recite the Creed,

* See *The Christian Preacher*, Part I, Chapter V.

and made him stop when he came to the clause,
' I believe in the forgiveness of sin.' ' Do you
believe that ? ' he said. ' Then put the word my
in; say ' I believe in the forgiveness of *my* sins.'
Pardon comes in the *appropriation* of the promise.
That comforted the storm-tossed soul, but only
for a moment." * But a renewed study of *Romans*
brought a more enduring assurance, " I sought day
and night to make out the meaning of Paul; and
at last I came to apprehend it thus; through the
Gospel is revealed the righteousness which availeth
with God—a righteousness by which God in His
mercy and compassion justifieth us; as it is written
' The just shall live by faith.' Straightway I felt
as if I were born anew. It was as if I had found the
door of Paradise thrown wide open. Now I saw
the Scriptures altogether in a new light—I ran
through their contents as far as my memory would
serve, and compared them, and found that this
righteousness was really that by which God makes
us righteous, because everything else in Scripture
agreed thereunto so well. The expression ' the
righteousness of God ' which I so much hated before,
now became dear and precious—my darling and
comforting word. That passage of Paul was to me
the true door of Paradise." † The distinctive theology of the Reformation sprang out of the personal
experience of Luther. When in Rome on the business of his order, " he visited all the oldest churches,
swallowed wholesale, he says, all the legends his

* *Luther and the German Reformation*, by T. M. Lindsay, pp. 35-36.
† Quoted *op. cit.*, pp. 36-37.

guides repeated to him; studied the ruins of ancient Rome; marvelled at the Colosseum and at the baths of Diocletian. Only once did his evangelical faith rebel against all this superstition. There was and is in Rome a great staircase, its steps worn with the pressure of thousands of pilgrims—the Holy Staircase, which was said to have once formed part of Pilate's house. An indulgence from penance for a thousand years is promised to those pilgrims who climb it on their knees. Luther began the ascent, repeating the usual prayers, but when he got half-way up, he remembered the text, ' The just shall live by his faith '; he rose from his knees, stood for a moment erect, and then slowly walked down again. But if Luther was still unemancipated from mediæval superstitions, his sturdy German piety and his plain Christian morality turned his reverence for Rome into loathing. The city, which he had greeted as holy, was a sink of iniquity; its very priests were openly infidel, and scoffed at the services they performed; the papal courtiers were men of the most shameful lives; he was accustomed to repeat the Italian proverb, ' If there is a hell, Rome is built over it.' It was much for him in after days that he had seen Rome for that month which he had spent in the papal capital." * Such was the first collision between the new life he had won and the religious superstitions and moral corruptions of Rome. Into the details of the conflict it is not at all necessary for our purpose to enter.

(*b*) It is with his preaching as a weapon which

* *Op. cit.*, pp. 43-44.

he wielded in the conflict that we are concerned. He had been able to preach learned discourses in the convent chapel, for there he had an audience that could appreciate them. When he undertook the duties of the preacher in the town-church of Wittenberg, he recognized that he must make himself understood by the "raw Saxons." And "the common people heard him gladly." The description of his preaching given by Dr. Lindsay is so good as a lesson for every preacher as to be worth quoting in full: " He spoke in plain nervous German. He gathered collections of German proverbs and country sayings, and used them as illustrations. He noted that our Lord used the homeliest illustrations, talking of tilling the ground, of mustard seed, of sparrows and sheep and fish; and he went and did likewise. It is impossible to misunderstand Luther's sermons. Above all, he had a way of making the Bible living, of showing that it was full of histories of men and women who had lived and talked and eaten and slept and married and given in marriage. All this was new. No matter what the text was, the sermon was sure to come round in the end to that doctrine of grace which he had first learned by the hearing of the ear at his mother's knees, then cast behind him in his student days, and finally got hold of again after sore conflict in Erfurt monastery—the doctrine of the radical distinction between the law and the Gospel—the doctrine that the divine righteousness is not mere punitive justice, but saving merit made over once for all to every believer in Christ—the doctrine that faith is not belief in propositions but a trust in, and a personal fellowship with, a crucified Lord." *

(c) One must fully acknowledge that Luther had his limitations. He was engaged with the Scriptures only in so far as he could find in them the Gospel of individual salvation; he resisted and rejected the beliefs and practices of Rome only in so far as these hindered and endangered the assurance of this salvation for the individual conscience; to advance the interests of the movement he was too subservient to princes; the excesses of fanaticism made him unduly conservative, and even intolerant. " As for Luther himself, the Peasants' War imprinted in him a deep distrust of the ' common man ' which prevented him from believing in a democratic Church, and led him to bind his reformation in the fetters of a secular control, to the extent of regarding the secular government as having a quasi-episcopal function. He did his best within Germany to prevent attempts to construct anything like a democratic church government." † Much in the relation of the Lutheran Church to the State, in the religious life, and the attitude of Christians to the Social Problem in Germany even to-day can be traced to the influence of Luther.

(d) Nevertheless the words of Harnack express the true estimate of Luther: " What an inexhaustible richness his personality included ! How it possessed in heroic shape all that the time most lacked—a

* *Op. cit.*, pp. 48-49.
† *Op. cit.*, p. 189.

wealth of original intuition which outweighed all the elements of culture in which it was defective; a certainty and boldness of vision which was of more value than any insistence on free investigation; a power to lay hold on what was true and to conserve what would stand the test of time compared with which the merely critical faculty is pointless and feeble; above all a wonderful ability to give expression to strong feeling and true thought, to be a *seer* and a *speaker*, to persuade by the written and spoken word as the prophet must do." *

II. It must not be forgotten that Luther was not the only leader of the Reformation. The broad river of Protestantism can be traced back to two sources—one in Germany and another in Switzerland.

(*a*) Ulrich Zwingli (1484-1531) was the leader of an independent movement. Not his was the personal experience of the joyous discovery after sore travail of soul of the secret of salvation; he passed from the Renaissance to the Reformation by the way of the study of the Bible and the Fathers; and by that study he was led to an even more decisive abandonment of Roman doctrine and practice. But his fame has been eclipsed by the second leader of the movement in Switzerland—John Calvin (1509-1564), although a similar personal experience to Luther's, of which we have, however, no record in detail, led him to be in closer sympathy with Luther than with Zwingli; or than Zwingli himself had been.

(*b*) A Frenchman by birth he placed himself in

* Quoted by Lindsay, *op. cit.*, pp. 264-265.

the front rank of the Reformation by the publication in Latin in 1536 of his *Institutes of Theology* as an apology for French Protestantism, a systematic treatment of Christian doctrine of a logical consistency such as Luther could never have produced and such as places him among the master minds in the exposition of Christian truth. It is with his preaching, however, and with the influence of that preaching that we are here concerned. His aversion to enter on public life, due to his love of study, was overcome on a visit to Geneva, only by " the terrible adjuration " of Farel, who claimed his help. " You have no other pretext for refusing me than the attachment which you declare you have for your studies. But I tell you, in the name of God Almighty, that if you do not share with me the holy work in which I am engaged, He will not bless your plans, because you prefer your repose to Jesus Christ ! " * Such a summons could not be resisted; and from that day onward, until the end of his life, except for a short exile, his preaching dominated the policy of Geneva. " He was distinguished among the Reformers for his zeal to restore again the conditions which had ruled in the Church of the first three centuries. . . . He recognized as none of them did that the Holy Supper of the Lord was the centre of the religious life of the Church, and the apex and crown of her worship. He saw how careful the Church of the first three centuries had been to protect the sacredness of the simple yet profound

* Beza's *Life* (old French edition), p. 22, quoted in Dargan's *History of Preaching*, Vol. I, p. 445.

rite; and that it had done so by preventing the approach of all unworthy communicants. Discipline was the nerve of the early Church, and excommunication was the nerve of discipline; and Calvin wished to introduce both. Moreover he knew that in the early Church it belonged to the membership and to the ministry to exercise discipline and to pronounce excommunication. He desired to reintroduce all these distinctive features of the Church of the first three centuries—weekly communion, discipline and excommunication exercised by the pastorate and the members. . . . Calvin's mistake was that while he believed that the membership and the pastorate should exercise discipline and excommunication, he also insisted that the secular power should enforce the censures of the Church. . . . Calvin's ideas, however, were never accepted save nominally in any of the Swiss Churches, not even in Geneva." * Not only was the idea of excommunication distasteful to the pastors and the people, but the magistrates of the Swiss republics thought it contrary to their dignity to be expected to carry out the behests of the ministry. In Switzerland Calvin did not get his ideas carried out to the full, but in the French Church, and partially in Scotland under the influence of John Knox, he had greater success. Calvin's insistence on his ideal in Geneva provoked a hostility which drove him and Farel into exile for a time. On his return he became the directing mind and controlling will, through his commanding voice, of the city.

* Lindsay's *History of the Reformation*, Vol. II, pp. 109-111.

(c) It became a centre of Protestantism. " Men with the passion of learning in their blood came from all lands—from Italy, Spain, England, Scotland, even from Russia, and above all, from France. Pastors, educated in Geneva, taught by the most distinguished scholars of the day . . . went forth from its schools to become the ministers of the struggling Protestants in the Netherlands, in England, in Scotland, in the Rhine provinces, and above all, in France." * Thus Calvin's theology gained a wider range than Luther's, and owing to his distinctive teaching, exercised a more direct and potent influence on the political structure of the societies which it reached; nations were moulded by his ideas.

III. One of the men influenced by Calvin, through whom Calvin's ideas made a nation, was John Knox (1505-1572).

(a) To his "natural character before it was moulded from without," A. Taylor Innes ascribes "insight and audacity, tenacity, tenderness, common sense, humour." As a student in Glasgow University he came under the influence of John Major, "who had brought from Paris a vast academical reputation." For nearly twenty years after this we know nothing about his history. In 1540 he appears as a notary and a priest in his native district, and in 1543 he describes himself as "minister of the sacred altar, of the Diocese of St. Andrews, notary by Apostolic authority." As he is spoken of as " Sir John " we may assume that

Op. cit., p. 133.

he had taken the master's as well as the bachelor's degree at the University. In 1546 he had identified himself with the cause of Wishart, then already on point of suffering martyrdom for the cause of the Reformation. A year later Knox himself is denouncing the Pope " as the official head of an Anti-Christian system." * How this rapid change was brought about we do not know, as Knox himself was very reticent about his inner life at this period.

(b) He was one of the party who held the Castle of St. Andrews after Wishart's martyrdom, and the assassination of Cardinal Beaton. " Here by what we may call a stratagem, he was induced to enter on the public exercise of the Christian ministry, and such power accompanied his sermons and disputations during his seven months of residence in the place, that a good number of the inhabitants renounced Popery, and made profession of the Protestant faith by partaking together of the Lord's Supper. The circumstance is memorable on this account, that then for the first time the sacrament was dispensed in Scotland in the scriptural way." † When, invested by a French fleet, the castle was surrendered, Knox was with others sent to the galleys in France. He refused to offer adoration to a wooden image of the Virgin, and threw it into the water. The intervention of Edward VI assured him his liberty again, and he had some share in the work of the Reformation in England. When Mary

* *John Knox*, pp. 10-13.
† Walker's *Scottish Church History*, p. 29.

came to the throne he had to retire to the Continent. After some years' wanderings he settled down in Geneva as pastor of the English congregation there.

(c) His intimacy with Calvin exercised a decisive influence over him. A brief visit to Scotland in 1555-56 convinced him that the country was not yet ready for any great movement. After the adoption of the First Covenant in 1559 he returned to Scotland; and until his death in 1572 was the virtual ruler of the nation, and laid broad and deep the foundations of the Reformed Kirk of Scotland, which has exercised over the thought and life of the Scottish people as great an influence as, even if not a greater than, any Church in any land. He was not, however, mainly a statesman, great as are his services in this sphere. He remained a diligent student, giving much care to the preparation of his sermons. He preached twice every Sunday, and three times during the week, and the congregation sometimes numbered thousands. The administration of the newly established Church largely depended on him. His pastoral work, dealing with individual souls, made large demands not on his time only, but on heart and mind. While Edinburgh was the centre of his activities, he often went on preaching tours throughout the country.

(d) A sentimental admiration for Mary Queen of Scots, which her lamentable career does not justify, has led those who have not studied the history of the period to feel a prejudice against

John Knox. In his contest with her he was not only defending freedom of conscience in religion, but opposing what aimed at being a political despotism. Had the reformer not withstood the Queen face to face, had he not publicly by appeal to the nobles and the people in his preaching thwarted her schemes, the cause of progress would have suffered defeat. The victory of Protestantism in Scotland was made sure by the horror awakened by the crime of France in 1572, the massacre of St. Bartholomew. John Knox's confidence that his life-work had not been in vain is expressed in a message he sent to " Mr. Secretary Cecil " through the English envoy Killigrew: " John Knox doth reverence your Lordship much, and willed me once again to send you word, that he thanked God that he had obtained at His hands, that the Gospel of Jesus Christ is truly and simply preached throughout Scotland, which doth so comfort him as he now desireth to be out of this miserable life."* John Knox's care for the education of the people must not be forgotten; although he was hindered in accomplishing all he desired for the common good by the selfishness of the nobles. He had to contend not only against avowed enemies but also against professed friends; but he endured as seeing Him who is invisible. He " never feared the face of man," because he ever walked in " the fear of God."

It was " truth through personality " which in Martin Luther changed Germany, in Calvin Geneva, and in John Knox Scotland. The Reformation in

* Quoted by Taylor Innes, *op. cit.*, p. 143.

England lacked any commanding prophet; and, such as it was, was brought about by political action. Although not of the same stature as these three men, and having a much more restricted range of influence, Hugh Latimer (about 1490-1555) deserves mention as an effective popular preacher, and as a martyr to his faith. His encouragement to his companion in death was a sure word of prophecy: " Be of good comfort, Master Ridley, and play the man; we shall this day light such a candle by God's grace in England as I trust shall never be put out."

No historical movement has owed as much to preaching as the Reformation; and if the light then kindled is never to be put out, it must be kept bright by the same agency. In the succeeding century and a half there is no name among Protestant preachers which can be placed beside these three as of equal importance and influence. But in the eighteenth and nineteenth centuries there were movements, the leaders of which claim our attention as illustrating historically that the Church lives as it adapts itself to the world in which it bears its witness, offers its worship, and does its work. These three movements are the Evangelical Revival under John Wesley, the revival of German theology under Schleiermacher, and the Anglo-Catholic revival under John Henry Newman, all of whom were conspicuous as preachers.

CHAPTER VI

THE REVIVAL PERIOD

AFTER the Reformation there was a marked decline in preaching in the Protestant Churches. Just as Judaism was a relapse to legalism and formalism from the inspiration of the prophets, so scholasticism reasserted itself after the moral and religious quickening of the Reformers in the dogmatism of their successors. One of the consequences of the Reformation, inevitable and nevertheless lamentable, was the division of the Church into churches, and the nationalism of these churches in spirit and outlook as well as in form. In England there was a distinct contrast during the seventeenth and eighteenth centuries between Anglican and Puritan, Churchman and Nonconformist; and in Scotland in the eighteenth and early nineteenth centuries between Evangelical and Moderate; but no preacher is so conspicuous as a creative personality as to deserve mention in this brief sketch.* In the seventeenth and early eighteenth centuries the Roman Catholic pulpit in France had its Augustan age of pulpit eloquence, and listening to sermons became a pastime of the Court.† Important as these

* See *The Christian Preacher*, Part I, Chapter VI.
† See *The Christian Preacher*, Part I, Chapter VII.

orators are in a study of preaching as an art, as expressing the growing life of the Church they can be passed over. In Germany in the same period pietism and rationalism stood in antagonism to one another; but there were also mediating personalities,* to the greatest of whom, Friedrich Daniel Schleiermacher, we must return, when we have dealt with John Wesley the outstanding religious personality of his age.

I. The Evangelical Revival † may in its influence be compared with the Reformation; for it affected the history of England politically as well as religiously and morally. It probably saved the country from an experience similar to that of the French Revolution; it brought moral cleansing and religious quickening to the common people throughout the length and breadth of the land; in it lie the sources of the broadening stream of philanthropic and missionary effort of the nineteenth century. While there were good and godly men in all the Churches, bearing their witness to the Gospel, and doing the work of the Church, yet it may without injustice be said that Church and Dissent alike did not display the enthusiasm or the energy of a community filled with the Holy Spirit. The tide of Christianity was at its lowest ebb, but it turned and became a full flood by the labours mainly of John Wesley (1703-1791), although George Whitfield was his fellow-worker.

* See *The Christian Preacher*, Part I, Chapter VIII.
† See *The Christian Preacher*, Part I, Chapter IX, pp. 211-220.

(*a*) His was no conversion from a godless to a godly life, as at Oxford he and his companions for their devout practices earned the nickname of Methodists, a name transferred to the evangelical movement with which this formalism had no kinship or likeness. Distressed in mind about his spiritual condition, Wesley found the relief and satisfaction which he had vainly sought by a scrupulous fulfilment of his duties as a clergyman in a recovery of the truth which had been Luther's discovery. The influence of Luther was mediated to him by the Moravian community in London, founded by Peter Böhler. He has himself described how the change, which made him the evangelist, was brought about, on 24th May, 1738. "In the evening I went very unwillingly to a society in Aldersgate Street, where one was reading Luther's preface to the Epistle to the Romans. About a quarter before nine, while he was describing the change which God works in the heart through faith in Christ, I felt my heart strangely warmed. I felt I did trust in Christ, Christ alone, for salvation; and an assurance was given me, that He had taken away my sins, even *mine*, and saved *me* from the law of sin and death." He now personally realized with intellectual certainty and emotional confidence a truth he had already known and taught, but not made fully his own.

(*b*) Sharing with the Moravians the doctrine of justification by faith, he did not accept their quietism, but insisted that faith must bear fruit in works. Rejecting the doctrine of election of Calvinism, and accepting the Arminian doctrine of free will, he insisted on the necessity of the Spirit's operation in justification and sanctification alike. The distinctive features of his theology have been stated thus by Fisher.* "This faith in the living power of the Holy Spirit, not anything ascribed to unaided human agency, was the secret of the emphasis which was laid on Assurance as a privilege attainable by all believers. From the same source sprang the Wesleyan doctrine of Perfection. All believers may attain to a perfection, which, however, is not a *legal* but a *Christian* perfection. It is a state in which love to God and man reigns continuously, where there are no presumptuous sins, yet where there are still involuntary negligences and ignorances, transgressions of the perfect law, for which, therefore, forgiveness through the Atonement is requisite." It is this double certainty which explains why Wesleyan Methodism can be described as "Arminianism on fire." There is the danger of self-deception, a self-confidence which neither the spiritual condition nor the moral character justifies; but it must be conceded that such a certainty that God has forgiven and is making holy by His own Spirit will not only be emotionally satisfying, but be invigorating for the will.

(c) Wesley's innate conservatism was overcome only by the necessity which circumstances laid upon him. Refused admission to the churches, he very reluctantly yielded to Whitfield's persuasion, and preached in the open-air; and this ministry he

* *History of Christian Doctrine*, p. 392.

continued for fifty-two years. He was no less hesitant about adopting the agency of lay-preaching; he allowed Thomas Maxfield, a companion and servant of his brother Charles, to preach, only when convinced that the Spirit of God had chosen him for an agent. " It is the Lord," he confessed, " let him do what seemeth Him good." He remained a loyal churchman, and delayed as long as possible doing anything that would bring about an irretrievable breach; but at last he had to make provision for the continuance of the work he had begun; by the class-meeting he secured the pastoral care for his converts. The Church of England did not know the day of her visitation, and missed a God-sent opportunity for the renewal of her life, and the recovery of the common people for her ministries. But in view of what Wesleyan Methodism has grown to at home and abroad, it may be that the fulfilment of God's purpose in John Wesley depended on the disappointment of his own hopes. The sermons of John Wesley do not in themselves account for the extraordinary impression made and influence wielded; they are scholarly, thoughtful, earnest, searching and practical, but it was the Spirit-filled personality that made the truth effective unto salvation for multitudes.

II. While the Renaissance and the Reformation were contemporary, the Reformation was not as fully influenced by the Renaissance as would have been necessary to avoid the schism which has marked modern thought between, to use Tennyson's words, "faith" and "knowledge." Theology retained much that was mediæval, while science and philosophy were shaping the modern mind. The deists in England and France, and the rationalists in Germany show the opposition between intellectual development and dogmatic conservatism. Great as was the influence of the Evangelical Revival on religion, its contribution to theology is negligible; it did not help to bridge the gulf between piety and philosophy and science. It was necessary that the currents of the Reformation and Renaissance should be brought into one channel. Such a reconciliation meant a revival for theology, and as theology reacts on religion, even for religion. Although for "the man in the street" it may seem absurd to bring Friedrich Daniel Schleiermacher (1768-1834) into comparison with John Wesley, yet for the theological thinker his importance is not less.

(b) He combined in himself what in the thought and life of his age was widely separated. His piety was rooted in the education he had received at a Moravian school; his philosophy, and consequently his theology came to him from rationalist teachers at the university. He never completely harmonized his Moravian heart and his rationalist head; but his sincere and strenuous effort to reconcile in himself, and to reconcile for others these conflicting tendencies has had a permanent value for later developments in theology. "With the Moravians," says Dr. Selbie,* "Schleiermacher had close affin-

* *Schleiermacher*, pp. 2-3.

ities, and . . . owed them a deep debt. But his mind was too speculative and critical to accept guidance in religion from any man or body of men. He had all the passion of an Erasmus for liberty. He broke with the Moravians at an early stage in his career, though without disturbing his friendly relations with them, and joined the University of Halle. After a two years' course there he went out into the world and began his self-appointed task of 'attaining, by earnest research and patient examination of all the witnesses, to a reasonable degree of certainty and to a knowledge of the boundaries of human science and learning.' At Halle he had come under the influence of the philosophy and the theology of the Enlightenment (Aufklärung) and had studied Kant. These influences, working upon the early impressions derived from Herrnhut, determined quite clearly the bent of his own mind, and it is important to understand, as his biographer Dilthey points out, that this had taken place before he became acquainted with the Romantic School, or had studied Spinoza. . . . He owed much to these two sources of inspiration, but they were not original formative influences in shaping either his outlook or his method."

(c) While a chaplain in Berlin he published his *Speeches on Religion Addressed to its Cultured Despisers*. "The teaching of the *Reden* is altogether original. It marks the transition in German theology from a barren rationalism to a warmer and a more positive faith. To the younger men of the time it came as a prophetic message and helped them to rediscover in religion that which had a function and a value of its own independent of culture and criticism. . . . It was said to have ' made religion fashionable.' But in the Church it was viewed with suspicion as having caused too marked a breach with the past, and as showing pantheistic tendencies. The criticisms were not altogether unfounded." * In successive editions of this work modifications were introduced which not only showed a living and growing mind, but also a progress toward the more positively Christian theology of his later work on *The Christian Faith*. " Throughout this great book," says Cross,† " we may perceive the working of his profound conviction that creeds and all formal doctrines are only approximate and temporary expressions of religious experience and must ever be subordinated thereto. He endeavours on the one hand to do justice to traditional and current dogmatical statements by bringing into relief the religious reality that lies behind them and, on the other, to indicate the limitations of their worth." While his two main writings have been specially referred to, it was not as a writer solely that he influenced his generation. " As a preacher he has had few, if any, superiors in Germany. Old Trinity church has become famous as the place where thousands felt the thrill of his warm, attractive personality and those stirring appeals that found their way into so many hearts. W. Robert-

* *Op. cit.*, pp. 4-5.
† *The Theology of Schleiermacher*, p. 59.

son Nicoll quotes a German writer as saying that 'thousands were won by him to the Saviour.' Many others received through him a deeper spiritual life." * We have good reason then for remembering him among the agents of the Spirit of God who have brought "times of refreshing from the presence of the Lord." A similar work, though of narrower range, was done in England by Frederick William Robertson (1816-1853) of Brighton.†

III. Whatever one's theological or ecclesiastical affinities may be it is impossible not to recognize the personal greatness of John Henry Newman (1801-1890),‡ or to deny the widespread influence which he has exercised upon his age. John Wesley emphasized individual experience, the conversion of the soul by the grace of God in Christ. Schleiermacher was concerned with the individual religious consciousness, and the significance of Christ for its redemption from the world unto God. In both the significance of the Christian society was secondary. What Newman did was to revive the authority and the influence of the Church. We may regret that the revival was a reaction, that he tried to stem the tide of progress by seeking to set up the bulwark of Patristic and Mediæval doctrine and practice, and that as a result of the Tractarian movement, of which he was the most inspiring leader, so large

* Op. cit., pp. 60-61.
† See The Christian Preacher, pp. 251-253.
‡ Op. cit., pp. 242-245.

H

a section of the Church of England has been impelled away from Protestantism towards Catholicism, and even in part at least Catholicism of the Roman type. But that there was need that the idea of the Church in its unity and universality should be revived within Protestantism cannot be doubted. The individualist type of Christianity has defects which need the correction of the revival of the consciousness of fellowship in the Christian society. This reason, as well as his personal greatness, justifies the mention of Newman here.

(a) His personal distinction, his dominating influence, the charm and the power of his preaching have been described by Sarolea in his book *Cardinal Newman*. I shall here call another witness, and one by no means so friendly. Of the *Apologia* in which the man is fully disclosed, Pfleiderer* says: "This autobiography owes its attractiveness not only to the universally acknowledged beauty of its style, but also to the honest openness with which the author describes the various phases of his religious opinions. A sincerely religious character is unveiled, as it struggles to reach the certainty of conviction with deepest earnestness; and if the appearance of ambiguity and want of sincerity sometimes arises, it is not from the slightest wish to conceal anything from others from external considerations, but because the writer is not clear in his own mind and because he is trying to hold perforce what is untenable and to conceal from

* *Development of Theology*, pp. 362-363.

himself consequences that are inevitable. But honourable as such a character may be, its weak side cannot be overlooked. The weakness consists rather in a moral than an intellectual inability to distinguish between religion and a particular form of its transmission in doctrine and ritual; because the firm centre of religious and moral certainty cannot be found in the man himself, he clings to external authorities, maintains vehemently their inviolability, and all the time is driven further and further by the inevitable feeling of their insufficiency, until, weary of searching and enquiring, the secure haven of Romish infallibility is at last resorted to."

(b) Is not this inner tragedy the explanation of the influence which Newman exercised in his own generation in and beyond Oxford ? The *Zeitgeist* was incorporated in him; he was the voice of an age of transition, when the old anchors having slipped, many souls were like a bark driven hither and thither by wind and wave; and he, uncertain of his own course, yet steered others into what was for them a welcome haven. Convinced as we may be that, launching out into the deep, and confronting the storm would have been the better choice for him and for those whom he influenced, we must nevertheless recognize that he was one of the most influential personalities in the Christian pulpit of last century.

The three preachers who have been chosen for mention in this chapter, when we present them to our minds together, suggest the consideration that what our age needs is the reconciling of the religious tendencies, which they may be taken as representing. Individual experience through faith in the grace of God is imperative; for the interpretation of that experience to make it convincing for the mind as well as satisfying to the heart there must be philosophical and theological knowledge and insight which can relate the experience to the total reality of thought and life; and such an interpreted experience needs for its fullest content and widest range membership in a community, in which the inheritance of the past is not a hindrance but a furtherance to fresh conquests in the present as the promise of still richer possessions in the future.

CHAPTER VII

THE MISSIONARY PERIOD

As the Evangelical Revival was the glory of the eighteenth century, so has the Foreign Mission Enterprise been of the nineteenth; and it would be impossible in dealing with the preachers of the Living Church to leave unmentioned the missionaries; but another treatment than that adopted in the previous chapters commends itself as the more suitable, as preaching is only one of the manifold agencies which have been used, and neither among the missionaries nor among their converts would it be possible to make a selection of only a few conspicuous among their fellows as preachers.* It will rather be more advantageous to distinguish three types of missionaries, and three stages of the work of missions.

I. The three types which we may distinguish are the scholar, the adventurer, and the pastor.

(i) It would be impossible to estimate the debt that scholarship owes to the missionary of the first type. To the knowledge of languages, to the comparative study of religions, to anthropology and

* See *The Christian Preacher*, pp. 230-240 ; and *History of Christian Missions*, by C. H. Robinson.

ethnology, only to mention those branches of scholarship most closely related to the work of missions, missionaries have contributed abundant and valuable material. They acquired the language of the people to whom they came in the name of Christ, and in many cases were even the first to reduce it to writing, and to furnish it with a grammar. They translated the Christian Scriptures, and some were not content to translate a translation, but went to the original. They acquainted themselves with the Sacred Scriptures of the ancient religions of civilized peoples; and in some cases in their knowledge put to shame the native scholars; and they disclosed the treasures in these writings to the scholars in Christendom. Among savage peoples they observed beliefs, rites, customs, and institutions, and so supplied the data for the consideration of anthropologists. While in the eighteenth century there were messengers of the Gospel, the world-wide movement of the nineteenth century was begun with William Carey (1761-1834), who gave it its watchword: " Expect great things from God; attempt great things for God." For fifty-one years without break he laboured at Serampore in Bengal, and by his scholarship and his educational activities, no less than by his preaching, gave a broad and firm basis to missions in India. Similar was the work of Alexander Duff (1806-1878), who by means of a liberal education in the English language secured a deep and lasting influence over high-caste Hindus, who in turn became a leaven within Indian society. To the same type of missionary belonged the pioneer of modern missions in China, Robert Morrison (1782-1834). Whether he was led by force of circumstances or by his own inclinations to the kind of work he did for twenty-seven years, it was as a scholar that he opened the way for the entrance of Christianity into China. He had a worthy successor in James Legge (1815-1897), who translated the Chinese classics into English, and spent the last years of his life in Oxford as Professor of Chinese language and literature. Combining the scholar and the adventurer Henry Martyn (1781-1812) burned out for God with a pure and bright flame. He was alike on fire in gaining knowledge and winning souls. As soon as he landed as chaplain in Calcutta, he threw himself with ardour into the study of Hindustani, Hindi, Persian, and Arabic; and had within five years translated the New Testament into Hindustani; journeying on to Persia in a few months he translated the greater part of the New Testament into Persian. His body could not sustain such ardour of the soul, and he died at Tokat in Asia Minor. Many other names might be placed on the roll of fame; but these will suffice to show that in this enterprise there is room for, and need of the scholar.

(ii) There is a romance of missions. Geographical exploration is one of the accompaniments of the missionary adventure. There have been missionaries who could not remain in one place, but must needs be pressing on to the regions beyond. Even if they were impelled thereto by natural inclination, that was cleansed of any unworthy motive, and hallowed for the worthiest ends by their personal devotion to Jesus Christ as Saviour and Lord. One of the early missionaries of the London Missionary Society, John Williams (1795-1839), gave voice to the spirit of these missionary adventurers in the words: " For my part, I cannot content myself within the narrow limits of a single reef." Like the apostle " in journeyings often, in perils in the sea," he carried the Gospel from island to island in the South Seas; and used the converts he won as messengers to spread the Gospel far and wide. On the 20th November, 1839, John Williams, with two other missionaries, landed in Erromanga where Captain Cook had been in danger of losing his life. The natives attacked them; he and one of his companions were brutally murdered, and their bodies dragged away for a cannibal feast. Another martyr missionary of the South Seas was James Chalmers, known and loved as " Tamate " by the islanders and a friend of Robert Louis Stevenson, who gave the measure of the man in the words, " he is as big as a church." He too was slain in New Guinea on April 7th, 1901. Wandering hither and thither among the nomad Mongols for twenty years (1870-1891), James Gilmour endured untold hardships and had few encouragements; yet he never lost heart or hope, and even more lived than preached Christ. Greatest of all these adventurers in fame, and not unworthy of the fame, was David Livingstone (1813-1873). It is not with him as one of the world's greatest explorers that we are now concerned; but as in all his labours and perils always, as he desired to be, a missionary, and greater as a Christian even than as a missionary. How he regarded the relation of his work as explorer and as missionary he himself has stated: "The end of the geographical feat is but the beginning of the missionary enterprise." Alone among his native companions, he was yet not alone, for, as he was assured, Christ was with him as he died upon his knees at Ilala. That spot will remain a sacred place for the Christian heart, an inspiration of the service and sacrifice which will consecrate the "dark Continent," for which he lived, laboured, suffered, and died.

(iii) The conspicuous illustrations of the third type of missionary, the pastor, is David Livingstone's father-in-law, Robert Moffat (1795-1883), who for nearly fifty years remained with one tribe, the Bechuana in South Africa. Not only did he translate the whole Bible into the Sechuana, and train a number of native evangelists; but he made his missionary station in Kuruman one of the most influential centres of Christianity in South Africa. He was spared for thirteen years after his return to England, and sustained interest at home in the land he so loved. For fifty years Griffith John (1831-1912) made Hankow the centre of an expanding evangelization; and he spread the Gospel by his pen no less than by his lips. With these veteran workers we may associate the name of one who in fifteen years amid trial, sorrow, care, labour, and peril laid the foundations of a Church which may be regarded as one of the most glorious triumphs of the Gospel—MacKay of Uganda. During most of these years he had to sustain the faith, courage, and hope of his converts through fiery persecution, although he himself marvellously escaped the oft-threatened martyrdom; worn out with what he had endured he died in 1890, having truly laid down his life. Within twenty years of his death there were 70,000 Christians in Uganda; that kingdom is a bright spot amid the surrounding darkness of Central Africa.

II. In the history of the missionary enterprise it is convenient to distinguish three stages, which are not strictly successive in time, as in the same mission the three stages may be simultaneous. The first stage may be described as *evangelization* ; the Gospel is preached in word and deed, service and sacrifice, and converts are won. Of the second we may speak, using the language of the New Testament as *edification* ; the converts must be gathered into Christian fellowship, must be instructed in Christian faith and duty, must be guided in the Christian Way, and guarded against the peril of lapsing into heathenism again, must be taught and trained to become witnesses and messengers of the Gospel themselves, must have their families brought up in the nurture of the Lord, and must under the guidance of the missionary learn the rudiments of self-government and self-support in their church life and work. The third stage may be called *emancipation*. It must be the aim of the missionary to encourage and assist such a development in moral character, religious experience, wisdom for the guidance, and power for the performance of the work of the Church of Christ among the native Churches that he will himself become unnecessary; and will be able confidently to commit both tasks of evangelization and edification to those whom he has himself brought through these two stages unto such maturity in Christ that thay are fit for emancipation.

(i) It is to the first stage of missions that for most Christians the greatest interest attaches. There is more glamour about the task of leading men out of the darkness of superstition and corruption into " the marvellous light " of the Gospel, " the glorious liberty of the children of God," than in the two other tasks; and there is still need in all mission lands for evangelization. When we compare the methods of the early missionaries with those of these later days, we shall discover how much experience teaches. It is not unjust to affirm that the early missionaries went out with the assumption that what they had to encounter was a religion entirely false, and that they must seek to replace it by the Gospel exactly as they themselves knew it in their own sectarian interpretation. During the century a twofold discovery was made by the more sympathetic and intelligent missionaries. On the one hand, there was a growth of respect for the religious beliefs and rites of the heathen; amid these was discovered what Tertullian called the *anima naturaliter Christiana* or movement of the soul toward God which might be used as a preparation for the presentation of Christ. On the other there was a loss of confidence in the absolute infallibility of the sectarian presentation of the truth and grace of Christ. Hence evangelization to-day for the missionary who knows his business means a search for the points of contact for the Gospel in his hearers, and an endeavour to detach himself as far as he can from the denominational or other limitations of his own apprehension of that Gospel, so that he may as far as possible remove every obstacle to, and secure every opportunity for conveying to others the reality of the Saviour and Lord, of whose revealing truth and redemptive grace he seeks to be an open channel. The tendency to-day is to use every means of stripping the preaching of the Gospel of any foreign dress, and of clothing it in native garb. To give one illustration, a missionary of musical taste and talent has adapted not only Indian tunes, but even Indian songs to Christian uses. The need and the duty of adaptation to time and place are being now more generally recognized.

(ii) Evangelization is but the beginning of the work. While generalizations are often dangerous, there is adequate evidence to justify the statement that the convert easily won is hard to keep, and the convert hardly won is easy to keep. A high-caste Hindu can be brought to confess Christ only with great difficulty and much delay; but when once the step has been taken there is not much danger of turning back. But in mass movements, however

great the care in preparation for baptism, conversion
usually means a less radical change, and so the work
of edification assumes greater urgency. Here too
there has been change of outlook. In the beginnings
of the native Churches the Christian type was too
imitative, and lacked independence; the missionary
might even make the mistake of reproducing too
closely abroad the conditions of the home Church
with which he was most familiar, even when such
adaptation of European, or even British, ways was
not the best course to secure that the structure of
the Church rested on the broad and deep foun-
dation of what was fit and worthy in the native
thought and life. From this tendency there was
a reaction to another extreme. Some native Churches
were abandoned to their own resources too soon;
and have shown by a serious relapse from Christian
standards of character and conduct that the thorough
Christianizing of a community won from heathenism must be a slow, laborious, and even painful
process. The habits, tastes, institutions of a community cannot be changed in one generation.
Sufficient as is the grace of Christ for a moral and
religious transformation, it is a developed personality such as Paul's that alone can exercise the faith
which proves its sufficiency; and even he needed
to be reminded of the resources at his command
(2 Cor. xii, 9). It will be seen what is the kind
of preaching, combined with personal pastoral care,
which is necessary to bring a community even of
genuine and earnest converts out of the infancy of
Christian life into its maturity. Paul's letters show

how even elementary morality has to be enjoined with all the authority that the father in God can command. Different as are the conditions at home, might not the preacher in a Christian land discover the need of just such edification in the Christian life?

(iii) A mistake is made and a wrong is done when this tutelage is carried on longer than it need be. One result of the War has been the stimulation of the spirit of nationalism, a revolt against European domination. In India, China, and Japan, the superiority which the European often assumes as his exclusive prerogative is being challenged. Even the Christian Churches are affected by the spirit of the times, and are claiming an independence for which often they are not as fit as they think they are, and which it is not easy for the missionary, accustomed to receive deference, and solicitous about the undoing of the work of many years, to concede. It is evident that risks must be run, sacrifices made, anxieties faced; the movement may be guided by wisdom and love; it cannot be arrested by authority, still less by any financial pressure. It may be that this task of emancipation will test the missionaries in regard to their discernment, disinterestedness, and courage even more than the two other tasks have done. The Spirit of truth will guide into the truth; but the truth must come to these native Churches through the personality of him who, having been father and master, is willing to be brother and servant.

If the missionary succeed in making himself

superfluous, because within these Churches there will arise preachers, teachers, leaders, no less faithful to the Gospel, and yet more fitted to interpret it to the thought, and apply it to the life of their own people, how bright the prospect of even more gracious and blessed pages in the history of the preachers of the Living Church, when the genius and ethos of peoples and races as yet unheard will find its distinctive expression in the proclamation of the one Gospel. In the second section of this volume the endeavour will be made to describe what the Christian preacher in our own land must be, worthily to fulfil his calling. This brief description of the present situation in the mission field, despite its perils full of promise, opens to him a wider horizon, the vision of which should hearten him for the nearer demands and duties.

PART II

PRACTICAL COUNSELS

CHAPTER I

THE PREACHER AND THE BIBLE

I. THE Christian Church preserves its identity through all the lapses of time and the changes of history. Despite differences of creed, code, and ritual there is a continuity of Christian thought and life ; the believer of to-day is in the same community of faith, hope, and love as the prophet or the apostle. The inner bond is the one Spirit of God, but there is no outer bond of larger significance and higher value than the Bible. The preacher may sometimes chafe at the custom of taking a text for every sermon. While it should not be allowed to become a bondage, yet there is reason for the custom. It is an indication that the preacher is not speaking by his own authority, or even in the name of a society, but that his message is rooted in, and grows out of the historical revelation of God and redemption of man, of which the Bible is the record, both testimony to fact and interpretation of truth.* The duty of relating the preaching of to-day, however closely it may be adapted to present needs and tendencies, to the

* See *A Guide to Preachers*, First Section, for an answer to the question, *How to Study the Bible*.

Bible, was never more imperative, because not only is its authority for doctrine and practice more generally neglected, and even more confidently challenged, but even among intelligent Christian people there is perplexity and even distress as to its meaning and value. The difficulty of dealing with the Bible in the pulpit, as modern scholarship demands that it should be dealt with, is very great, because of the divided opinion in the Churches in regard to the claims of that scholarship.

(1) It is a common complaint that the Bible is less read even by Christian people than it once was ; this is a matter on which precise information is not obtainable. That the Bible is less read as an obligatory and even meritorious duty must, I think, be admitted. But there seems to be no doubt that there is a more wide-spread interest in the intelligent study of the Bible, because there is a much greater demand for books about the Bible which will make it intelligible. The depreciation of reading books about the Bible instead of reading the Bible itself, is often due to an un-intelligent superstition ; to read the Bible without understanding it has no mysterious virtue ; and it is all to the good that so many are wanting to understand what they read. To read about the Bible will promote an intelligent reading of the Bible. The ignorance of, and revolt against the Bible outside of the Church compel the Christian preacher not only to take up the challenge bravely, but to deal with its authority, frankly basing its claims on intelligible grounds. While there are

many Christian people who hold the older views about its inspiration, and a few of them are at present very vocal, there are not a few who know enough about modern scholarship to have lost their confidence in its authority, but not enough to have found their confidence restored, as assuredly by adequate knowledge it would be restored.

(2) It is this divided state of opinion in the churches which creates the difficulty for the preacher. It is not just, at least to the majority of Christian ministers, to charge them with dishonesty and cowardice, because they do not proclaim in the pulpit what they have learned at college, and are still learning in their studies. As one who by some of his brethren may be regarded as too outspoken in all such matters, I want to urge some considerations in their defence.

(a) A minister who is appreciative and sympathetic towards the religious life of his people, will shrink from saying or doing anything that would give needless pain. He may regard as prejudices what some hold as principles, but he must always be respectful to sincere conviction. However mistakenly, for many genuine saints the certainties of the Gospel which the minister shares with them have been bound up with views about the Bible from which they cannot yet detach them, as he has happily been enabled to do. In whatever way he presents modern scholarship in the pulpit, it is his duty to allay these fears, and to assure the " timid saints " that he holds these certainties with the same intense convictions as they do, and that they can be detached from these or those views about the Bible. If a man knows this scholarship as he ought, he should be able to present it in such a way as to make the Bible even more precious than it has been, so that his hearers will be made to feel that there is more gain than loss in abandoning the older views and accepting the newer. Iconoclasm is a provocation of idolatry of the Bible, and not its correction. Honesty and courage need not be rash and rude.

(b) This plea cannot be offered for some of the champions of the older views ; they are often so offensive and intolerant that they do not deserve consideration, and even invite a chastisement by speech. When one of these champions describes brother-ministers who have laboured long and devotedly in the ministry of the Gospel as *blasphemers* (I have had that epithet applied to me myself), rebuke of their spirit is justified. Let these show consideration and courtesy who claim them. Yet even in such cases the preacher may hesitate. The harmony of spirit and concord of service are a sacred trust of the head of a Church. He must do all he can to promote peace, and to prevent conflict ; and the command of conscience must be very imperative to justify his saying or doing anything that would stir up strife. It may sometimes be in the highest interests of a Church that discordant elements should be removed ; but such a task demands a wisdom and a love which can be given only from above.

(c) Having said so much in favour of the policy

of caution and consideration, I must add that in
my judgment the duty of candour must be discharged, great as the difficulty may be. Many
have been estranged from the Church, and more
will be estranged by what they, not giving adequate
consideration to the difficulty of speech, condemn
as a criminal silence. Distrust of the Gospel
itself may result from the suspicion that its exponents
are not honest and courageous enough to utter
the truth they know. The verities that endure
unchanged may be disbelieved when the views
about the Bible with which they have been usually
associated have been abandoned. It is the tra-
ditionalists who are a far greater peril to the preservation of the Gospel for the thought and the
life of to-day than are even the negative critics.
But further, he who knows how his mind and life
have been enriched by modern scholarship in the
clearer meaning and the higher value given to
the Bible, will want to share his discovery with
others, especially when he knows that only as he
does so can he recover many well worth winning
from doubt or unbelief to faith. In the interests
of the Gospel itself, must the preacher make
the Bible known to others even as he himself
knows it.

II. The duty having been asserted of relating
preaching to the Bible, while the difficulty of
relating it to the Bible as modern scholarship
presents it has been recognized, the question
arises : How is this duty to be done, and this
difficulty to be met ?

(1) It seems so obvious as to appear unnecessary to insist that the preacher must qualify himself for the task ; and yet experience shows that, like many obvious things, this is often overlooked. The qualification is twofold ; the preacher must, on the one hand, be thoroughly familiar with modern scholarship, and on the other hand he must be very much at home in the Gospel.

(a) As regards this scholarship, " a little knowledge is a dangerous thing." An inadequately informed man is likely to be attracted by extreme views. Some of the boldest champions of Modernism in the pulpit show a readiness to adopt negative conclusions which a sound and reverent scholarship does not support. While the Christian preacher may not be able to probe any of the problems to the bottom for himself, it is well for him to be guided by not extreme but moderate opinion among scholars. While he will not cling to an opinion that most scholars have abandoned, he will not snatch at any opinion which only one or two scholars may advance. He will wait for, and trust in the general *consensus* and not commit himself to individual conjectures. If he can give adequate study to any question, he may be justified in offering an independent judgment, but otherwise he had better follow those who move slowly and yet surely. The reaction against extreme views which we have witnessed as regards, for instance, the Gospels, justifies this cautious attitude.

Further it must be insisted that the knowledge of the Bible must be as a whole. Opinions, however modern, about this or that book must not be simply borrowed. The preacher should have done enough study to know how his whole attitude in handling the Biblical material must be altered. This is the reason why a knowledge of the original tongues—Hebrew and Greek—is a qualification which the preacher should strive to attain. I had a teacher who after middle age passed from the traditional to the historical view ; but even in his teaching it was manifest that he was not at home in it, and that its methods were external to his mode of thinking. Lastly, it is only this intimacy that enables a man to discover the real value of the Bible as the record of the progressive revelation of God to man completed in Jesus Christ as Son and as Saviour. The preacher will make a false impression who simply passes on this new knowledge to his hearers as a matter of duty, it may even be with a sense of loss. If his own theology is not enlarged and enriched by this modern scholarship, if the value of the prophets, the apostles, and even Christ Himself, is not enhanced by this fresh understanding, he will probably do more harm than good. He has no right to rob his hearers of their goodly pearls, unless he can offer them in exchange the pearl of great price (Matt. xiii. 45, 56)—God more fully disclosed and more clearly seen in the Bible than ever before. The preacher must realize his obligation, always to enrich, and not to impoverish his hearers intellectually and spiritually.

(*b*) The second qualification of the preacher

who is dealing with the Bible from the modern standpoint is that he should be at home in the Gospel. By the Gospel I do not mean any narrow, rigid doctrinal scheme, nor would I restrict the Gospel to what is taught in the Gospels, or to what Paul called " my Gospel." Although in controversy Paul opposed the law of the Old Testament and the Gospel of the New, the Old Testament is not merely law, it is Gospel also. Dr. Bruce in one of his earlier works, *The Chief End of Revelation*, showed that God's action in history under the old as under the new covenant was *redemptive*. The Exodus from Egypt, and the Return from the Exile, and many a national deliverance between, present God as Saviour. What I mean then as the Gospel is the whole of the redemptive revelation of God, the representation of God not as Creator, Preserver, Ruler, and Lawgiver only, but as Father, forgiving, saving and blessing. This is Good News, and we miss the essential meaning of the Bible unless we find this meaning in it ; and we shall provoke prejudice, excite suspicion, and fail to convince unless we make people feel that this modern scholarship does not hide, but brings this Gospel into clearer light.

(2) In the discharge of the task there must be discrimination as to the method to be employed in different cases.

(*a*) There are a great many texts in regard to which it is not necessary to refer to questions of literary and historical criticism. It is possible to preach on one of the sayings of Jesus without expounding the Synoptic problem. A scholarly preacher runs the danger of exaggerating the importance of what as scholar he knows, and may even be eager to impart. The introduction to many a sermon is disproportionate, because the preacher makes this mistake. A safe rule is not to bring in any allusion to the findings of scholarship unless the exposition and the application of the text demand it ; but the preacher must not forget his scholarship, and for the sake of attractiveness or effectiveness in dealing with a text, deal with it in a way which he could not justify to his conscience as a scholar. To give some concrete instances, it would seem to me dishonest for a preacher to deal with a passage in Deuteronomy as the *ipsissima verba* of Moses, or to expound the twenty-third psalm as an expression of David's experience, or to enforce the teaching of John iii. 16 as the very words of Jesus Himself, or to base an evangelistic appeal on the mistranslation " almost thou persuadest me to be a Christian " (Acts xxvi. 28). Even if his congregation is illiterate as regards all such questions, he must not presume on their ignorance, or state from the pulpit what he would be ashamed to be convicted of saying if challenged by a scholar. Without explicit statement, the preacher in whose teaching scholarship is implicit will be gradually detaching his hearers from the erroneous opinions about the Bible.

(*b*) There are texts to which, however, justice cannot be done unless the historical situation is described. It is an incalculable loss to the preacher as well as to his hearers, if to avoid difficulty he shirks preaching on Isaiah liii. If he has any scholarship at all, he cannot simply assume that this is a direct prophecy of Christ and His Cross, although with " a conscience void of offence," he may bring his hearers at the close of his exposition to Calvary. It is not at all necessary for him to say that the author of this passage is not Isaiah of Jerusalem of the eighth century B.C. He need not discuss whether there is a Trito- as well as a Deutero-Isaiah, or whether the passages about the Servant were once a separate work. I do not think he need even discuss whether the prophet had Jeremiah or Zerubbabel before his mind. But let him simply assume that it is a prophet, sharing exile with his fellow-countrymen, who is seeking a solution of the problem of God's providence involved in his nation's suffering and shame, and who finds that solution in the principle that Israel as a martyr nation can be God's missionary to the other nations, or even more broadly that the suffering of the righteous brings salvation to the wicked. He may then complete his message by showing that as Israel failed to rise to the height of this vision of its destiny, the vision became reality only in Christ as Saviour and Lord. Again, if he were dealing with one of the stories in Daniel, honesty it seems to me would demand that he should not treat it as authentic history, but as a story told after many days to cheer and comfort in a time of persecution. Once more in dealing with a passage in the Fourth Gospel, such as John iii, a preacher might show how verses eleven to twenty-one are reflections of the evangelist based on the reminiscences in verses one to ten. Such a treatment, not controversial but constructive, offered in a reverent spirit and considerate expression, would familiarize people with modern scholarship without disturbing their confidence in the Bible, or provoking their hostility. What the method of treatment should always aim at is an enhancement of the value of the Bible by bringing out more clearly and fully its real meaning.

(c) It seems to me, however, that in the present situation it is impossible not to deal more explicitly even with the subject. There is a theological reaction, and the advocates of traditionalism are not silent, but very clamorous. Their misrepresentations are so gross, and their intolerance so intolerable, that in the interests of truth and charity a correction and a defence must be offered. While undoubtedly the exposition of the Bible from the modern standpoint will both expose the error and rebuke the uncharitableness, it may be necessary on fit occasion to let perplexed yet intelligent people know what this abused Higher Criticism is, and that its conclusions do not at all endanger any reasonable and reverent faith. Not all preachers are competent for such a task ; and " fools must not rush in where angels fear to tread." But where there is competence, there is also responsibility. Possibly the Bible Class or the week-evening lecture are in most churches the best methods. Some of the older people may be distressed, and even estranged, although if the task is wisely and kindly discharged, even that need not be the result. But it is certain that the younger people will respond most gladly to the liberation from doubt and bewilderment that the knowledge of the Bible as it actually is will bring to them. Not only does the preacher then owe it to the truth honestly " to divide the Word of Life," but his " cure of souls " demands that he shall satisfy minds enquiring or perplexed as well as relieve hearts distressed. Whatever the cost may be, he must not for himself lose, or suffer his hearers to lose, the instruction and inspiration which comes from an enlightened and reverent intimacy with the Bible. The Church is weak as it neglects the Bible ; it is strong as it cherishes its study, for the Bible is infallible in its proper purpose, to bring God to men, and men to God.

III. The zealous but unwise defenders of the older views about the Bible by their distortions of what the modern scholarship teaches are doing untold mischief to the cause which they have undoubtedly at heart. When they argue, as ignorantly they do, that the newer views destroy the authority of the Bible, they discredit the Bible for many. Some become indifferent to the Bible, and excuse themselves by pleading that modern scholarship has disproved its claims. Others are put in " a strait betwixt two," they want to retain their reverence for the Bible, and yet they cannot believe that competent scholars can be such fools or rogues as the champions of traditionalism make them out to be. These questions should be discussed on grounds of scholarship only, without imparting any theological prejudice ; only thus can the truth be spoken in love. Controversy is out of place in the pulpit, but in the present situation it rests as a solemn obligation on the preacher to show by his treatment of the Bible in the pulpit how unjustified is any indifference, and how unnecessary is the perplexity. In presenting the Gospel he may also be showing how unchanged is the authority for the moral and the religious life of the Bible, and how inexhaustible its interest, and incalculable its value.

(1) It is probable that it is the Old Testament that has suffered most in the regard even of Christian men. Many Sunday School teachers, for instance, frankly express an aversion to Old Testament lessons. They cannot accept as immediate commands of God practices which the Christian conscience condemns, and yet they have not learned to overcome the difficulty by the recognition of the progressiveness of divine revelation, its necessary limitation by the hardness of men's hearts, even as Christ Himself did (Mat. xix. 8). I may be pardoned for referring to a book I wrote some years ago to meet this aversion, *The Old Testament in the Sunday School.* Of one chapter on *The Value of the Old Testament for the Christian To-day*, I venture to give a summary here. (i) " We cannot understand the New Testament unless we know the Old, for the preparation

does not pass away before, but passes into and becomes part of the consummation " (p. 73). (ii) " There is development of thought and life presented to us within the New Testament, yet the literature covers only two generations. . . ." " The literature of the Old Testament covers a millennium at least," and we can study progress in a far longer process, and this progress shows us God's method of education (pp. 73-76). (iii) " The history which is contained in the Old Testament has a value for the Christian of to-day not mainly as an accurate record of facts, but because it gives the standpoint of religion in regard to history " (p. 76). (iv) " This interpretation of human history as divine providence is given by the succession of prophets " who " do supplement the teaching of the New Testament ; and for the complete character and conduct their message of social duty as religious is essential " (p. 78). (v) " The book of Psalms does full justice to the spirit of devotion " and gives it an expression excelled in no other religious literature (pp. 79-80). (vi) The Wisdom literature has the interest of the struggle of the mind of man with the problem of the ways of God to man. " There is no part of the Old Testament that may not be of value to us " (p. 81). Modern scholarship puts at the command of the preacher resources of knowledge and understanding such as no previous age possessed.

(2) Amid the distresses and conflicts of the present hour men are turning to the teaching and example of Jesus as the only clue to guide them

out of the labyrinth ; and the preacher is wise who deals much and often with Christian ethics in modern applications. But what men are discovering is that the Greek moralists were wrong who thought that wisdom is virtue, that to know the good ensures the doing of it. Men need an adequate motive, and a sufficient power. It is the love of Christ which constrains ; it is the Spirit of God who empowers. The Christian duty can be done only as the Christian life is possessed. The confident and triumphant interpretation of that life in the New Testament is needed to nourish that life to-day ; because it can make real to men the love of Christ which constrains and the Spirit of God which empowers. He does not preach Christ completely who does not show what Christ did for, and made of a John, or a Paul. Only as the Bible is in all its range and variety expounded, can the Gospel be effectively preached as the power and the wisdom of God unto salvation.

CHAPTER II

THE PREACHER AND MODERN THOUGHT

IF, reverting to the biological analogy expanded in the Introduction, we regard the Christian Church as an organism, we may describe the Bible as the factor of heredity in its development, and the Modern World as the factor of environment. An organism lives only as it adapts itself to its environment, or its environment to itself ; for we must recognize the possibility of mutual action and reaction. The Church is, and cannot but be affected by the world, but it may and should also influence the world. While in human personality it is impossible to divide the mental process into thought, feeling, and will, and isolate one element from another, yet we may make a relative distinction between the cognitive and conative activity, the impression in knowledge, and the expression in action, the theoretical and the practical problem of any age, interrelated as they may be. Thus the environment of the Church with which we are concerned may be considered as having two aspects, and these may conveniently be expressed by the

146

terms *thought* and *society*. In this chapter we shall be dealing with the former, and in the next chapter with the latter.*

(1) The word thought is used here in the widest sense, to include both the discovery of facts, causes, laws and the discernment of truths—both science and philosophy. The term modern needs closer definition, for it may be used in a variety of senses. If as Christians we desire to emphasize the difference Christ has made we may think of the world as uninfluenced by Him as the ancient, and the world in which His influence has been introduced as the modern. If as Protestants we wish to preserve the use of the term *Ancient*, but desire to show the importance of the Reformation, we may speak of the intervening period as the *Mediæval*, and the world since as the *Modern*. If as men of our age we recognize that the influence of the Reformation, conjoined with that of the Renaissance, began to have general effect only in the eighteenth century, and became fully effective only in the nineteenth century, we shall think rather of these centuries as representing what we regard as modern. Great as may be our appreciation of Luther, we must feel that in his thinking he was still very largely mediæval, and Protestant scholasticism was certainly a reversion to type even more marked, because unrelieved by his spiritual genius. It is with the development of science as begun by

---

* See *A Guide to Preachers*, Fourth Section, pp. 273-325, for a similar discussion on *How to meet the Age*, in its intellectual doubts and difficulties.

Bacon, and of philosophy beginning with Descartes on the one hand, and the industrial revolution, resulting from the use of steam as motor power, and the consequent inventions of machinery on the other hand, that the Modern World with which we are immediately concerned begins.

(2) In using the term *modern* we express no judgment of value, but simply make a statement of fact. In calling any theory or practice modern we do not assume that it is necessarily superior to what we describe as ancient or mediæval, still less that it will not be proved inferior to later developments of thought and life. We simply affirm that it is the latest product of human history, from the influence of which we cannot detach ourselves. If the preacher to-day takes account of modern thought, it is not to accept all its findings without any discrimination, but to apply to it as appreciatively as he can the Christian standard of judgment. If he believes as he must that God is fulfilling His purpose in human history, he will, recognizing the danger of stagnation or retrogression by reason of human ignorance and perversity, yet assume that there has been progress, that the thought of to-day is coming nearer the truth than the thought of a former age, and that in the life of to-day the will of God is being done, if still very imperfectly, yet more effectively than in previous times. Avoiding both the *pessimism* which condemns the age as the worst that has ever been, and the *optimism* which lauds it as the best that it could be, he will with a safer judgment

commit himself to *meliorism*, the conviction that the world is getting better, although " the best is yet to be," and can be made better as the best is made the aim. He will not approach modern thought in a suspicious or a credulous attitude. He will not assume that it must be hostile to his Christian faith, but be confident rather that, as the Spirit of God moves in the thought and life of man, there will be much in it which will enable him to make the Christian Gospel more credible, because more intelligible to the men of his own time.

I. One of the most potent factors in the development of modern thought has been *physical science*.

(1) If we compare the knowledge of the world at the beginning of last century and again at the beginning of this, what a revolution there has been ! What has brought home to everybody how great the change has been is the application of science to industry, commerce, and even to amusements. The cinema and wireless bring to the eyes and the ears of all men the wonders which science has wrought in the command over physical forces that the knowledge of natural laws has given. That hypotheses of a former age are being displaced by others does not discredit science, as foolish theological apologists would have their dupes believe, because each of these generally accepted hypotheses was the most adequate explanation for the knowledge of the time and it prepared for, and made possible, the hypothesis which has superseded it, on account of the increase of knowledge.

Science rises on stepping stones of dead hypotheses to higher things. Einstein has not robbed Newton of his glory ; although his theory of relativity is modifying the Newtonian physics. The theory of Darwin to explain the origin of species may be superseded but his fame as an investigator of the facts of organic evolution remains undimmed. Science is step by step getting nearer to the ultimate mystery of the Universe, and as it advances the wall of partition between the material and the spiritual grows less opaque, and becomes more transparent, so that there are men of science who justify the venture of faith that behind the atom there is God.

(2) It may be argued that wonderful as is the record of science, the Christian preacher has no concern with it, and may ignore it. Against such a conclusion I offer three considerations. *First of all* the controversy with Fundamentalists proves that the findings of science cannot be ignored : we can adhere to the theory of the verbal inspiration of the Bible, only if we can prove these findings false ; and if they are true, we must modify our theory. *Secondly*, as regards the doctrine of God and Man, Christian theology and modern science find themselves on common ground ; while the Gospel in its essentials remains unaffected the theology which seeks to expound and defend the Gospel is challenged to modify some of its statements. *Thirdly*, God the Father of our Lord and Saviour Jesus Christ is also the Creator of the Universe ; and it is a loss to the religious life—

even the Christian—that God's relation to nature should be ignored. The religious interpretation of that relation is complementary to the scientific explanation of the universe ; and it is necessary that it should be offered in terms that do not appear contradictory. Each of these considerations may be more fully presented.

(i) If the Bible is an inspired encyclopædia, a divine guide to all knowledge, a text-book of every *'ology*, if there is a Biblical geology, biology, anthropology, and psychology, then assuredly we must speak of modern knowledge about nature and man as " science falsely so called " ; and every conclusion that this science offers must be taken up as a challenge of our faith. If, however, the Bible is the record of divine revelation and human redemption in the region of morality and religion, and has no concern with physical science which God has given man the capacity to develop for himself; if its purpose is to make "wise unto salvation " and to equip " the man of God for every good work"; and if in fulfilling that purpose the writers use the knowledge of their time, as they were bound to do in the exercise of their own intelligence, and that their words might be intelligible to others: then there need be no conflict between religion and science. It is this view which has been more fully dealt with in the previous chapter, and is assumed throughout this whole volume. In his last work, *Landmarks in the Struggle between Science and Religion*, Dr. James Y. Simpson has shown how disastrous to the real interests of religion has been this challenge of science in its own sphere by religion. Christian theology has been driven from one field of knowledge after another, which under a mistaken view of the Bible it had invaded. What is so harmful in these futile encounters is this, that the authority of the Church within its own proper province is discredited ; the Gospel is for many minds identified with ancient errors ; the Christian conscience is distressed, and Christian faith disturbed. Accordingly while it is not the duty of every Christian preacher to discuss these questions in the pulpit, although on those who have the competence the obligation may rest in special circumstances, the preacher, if he can, should make it clear that his Gospel is not bound up with any antiquated views, and does not challenge science in its own sphere.

(ii) There are, however, some matters on which Christian theology cannot but be affected by the conclusions of modern science ; and in dealing with these it will be necessary to consider biology as well as physical science. No attempt can be made to cover the whole ground, only one or two illustrations can be given.

(a) First of all a general consideration of very far-reaching significance must be presented. The Christian theologian who has allowed modern science to influence his thinking as he ought, will seek to correct the errors of the popular conception of God. That conception is still very largely deistic. God made and finished the world by a

series of acts of omnipotence many ages ago, but
He still intervenes and even interferes with its
natural order in His providence by miracles. Some
Christians have an insatiable appetite for the
marvellous, and set no bounds to their credulity.
What science presents to us is the Universe as an
evolving unity. Omnipresent are physical force
and natural law ; there is a continuity in change ;
there is a mutual dependence of all the parts.
If we are to believe in God at all, we must believe
in an immanent, active God, the Father, as Jesus
taught, working hitherto. Because it is God Who
works in physical forces according to natural
laws, the order of nature shows God's constancy ;
and we should not desire or expect divine interference in our private interests, although we may
believe in divine direction of the whole in His
individual solicitude on our behalf. While modern
science does not compel us to abandon the belief
in miracles, it does challenge us to scrutinize very
carefully every alleged miracle, to discover if there
is sufficient reason in the divine purpose as disclosed to us in Christ, and adequate, reliable,
historical evidence. The miracles of Jesus generally
do, I believe, stand these tests, but many of the
marvels alleged in the history of the Church,
and claimed by individual believers, do not. Modern
science is thus a useful corrective of credulity,
but need not be a dangerous contradiction of
faith, for the conception of God which it constrains
Christian theology to adopt satisfies the intelligence
and no less meets the moral and religious needs of men.

(*b*) Another error of popular thinking that this conception of God will correct, which is responsible for a great deal of ignorance and inactivity, is the assumption that all that occurs is by or according to the will of God. The results of human error or wrong-doing are often acquiesced in as the divine will ; evils which might be prevented by intelligent action are ascribed to a " mysterious dispensation of the divine providence," and resignation is regarded as the human duty. If we believe that God is a God of law and order, that His action is not arbitrary, that events are the consequents of their conditions, we shall not take refuge in mystery, but understanding the how and why of our experience, we shall trace evils to their sources, and discover that by removing the causes we can prevent the effects. God's constancy in the natural order is the condition of our being able to discover His purpose, and to co-operate in its fulfilment with Him. The preacher who does not pander to an unintelligent pietism in encouraging his hearers to be always discovering special providences in their own lives, but exhibits the intelligibility of God's regular working in and through nature, thus making possible a reasonable ordering of human life, will command the respect of all whom modern science has influenced, and at the same time encourage a much more sensible and practical type of Christian character. The good man who can trace any evil that comes into his life from natural or human causality will not dishonour God by ascribing it to

God's will, but will not the less seek to know and do God's will in the way in which he deals with the evil, making it, if possible, subservient to his own good and that of others. A preacher whose thinking has been disciplined by the exact methods of science will be a much safer and more helpful guide in the moral and religious life than the sentimentalist, who expresses any and every pious fancy ; his preaching will certainly be more adapted to the age.

(c) Modern science leads us to modify the conception of man to which Christian theology has often committed itself. One of the doctrines which has exercised a most pernicious influence in Christian thought and life is that of *original sin*. At the beginning of the war a popular preacher declared that one thing the war had taught us was the truth of this doctrine. One must suppose that he did not know what the doctrine really asserted ; or that he was ignorant of the contradiction of the doctrine by modern science. According to the teaching of the Protestant Confessions every babe born into the world is responsible for the transgression of Adam, the ancestor of the race, and is held guilty, liable to eternal damnation on that account, apart from any personal transgression. The transgression of Adam involves as its further penalty that each child inherits a totally depraved nature, and apart from renewal by the grace of God is incapable of any good. The first part of the doctrine challenges our sense of justice ; and the second offends our sense of truth. But we are now concerned with what science has to teach us here, for on the ground of the nature and the development of man, racial and individual, science is in the field as well as theology. It is not proved that acquired characters can be transmitted ; and it is therefore an assumption that the sin of the ancestor of the race can have changed the nature of man. It is quite inconceivable that one transgression can have produced such a disturbance of human nature as the doctrine assumes. There is a racial solidarity in time and space ; physical heredity, and probably still more social inheritance, and environment affect individual development ; the evolution at some point went wrong, and each child starts on his moral course with a handicap, for the animal appetites and impulses get the start of conscience, reason and affection, and education and environment instead of restraining often stimulate the tendencies to evil that lie in the revolt of the animal against the rational. That sin abounds, and that only the grace more abounding can save from sin is a truth the modern preacher can unhesitatingly declare, for human history and individual experience afford the evidence ; but when he preaches on sin, let him beware of using catch phrases that either have no meaning for his hearers or carry a false meaning, and let him base his argument and appeal on such facts as have just been mentioned. The complaint is often made that men to-day have not the sense of sin which they had ; are not the preachers responsible in some measure for that who have continued preaching doctrine which does not square with the facts as science discloses them ?*

(iii) A distinction is made between religions in regard to the good which they seek. At the lowest stage man seeks by his religion to obtain natural goods, and so he worships the spirits or gods who can, he believes, provide for his needs, or protect him from his dangers. A higher phase is reached when man begins to be concerned about goodness, and associates his morality with his religion, regarding the gods or God as the lawgiver and the Judge ; he now seeks forgiveness of his transgressions, and help in his submission. The highest phase is when man sees in God Himself his highest good, not in any gifts God may bestow, not even in what God by His grace may help him to become, but in personal communion with God, the joy of His Presence, the blessing of His favour. But in the highest phase the lowest is not superseded, but transformed. As Jesus taught in the Sermon on the Mount, the believer is not anxious for the morrow, not because he has ceased to have needs and dangers, but because he trusts the care and the bounty of the Heavenly Father (Matt. vi. 25-34). As in communion with God conformity to God is obtained, the moral problem is fully solved in the spiritual good.

(a) Many Christians, however, do not carry the whole reality of man's relation to God into their religion. I do not say that evangelical theology

* See Tennant's *The Origin and the Propagation of Sin,* and *The Fall and Original Sin.*

has been excessively preoccupied with the problem of sin and its forgiveness ; for we cannot take too serious a view of sin, or have too grateful a sense of forgiveness ; but I do say that it has been too exclusively concerned with what is but part, however important a part it may be, of man's relation to God. God is Creator as well as Redeemer, and Nature is a revelation of God as well as God's dealing with man's sin in grace. The Psalms are in this respect as in so many others a devotional guide. How many of the Psalms declare the glory of God in the heavens and His bounty on the earth ! Jesus too in His teaching shows what the Christian preacher often forgets, the presence and activity of the Heavenly Father in the birds of the air and the flowers of the field. Here Paul, great as he was, shows a limitation ; the sights and the sounds of nature seem not to have attracted his attention as did the ways and the works of men ; and yet even Paul teaches the people of Lystra that God "left not Himself without witness, in that He did good, and gave you from heaven rains and fruitful seasons filling your hearts with food and gladness " (Acts xiv. 17). It is not only at the harvest festival that town-dwellers especially need to be reminded of the ultimate dependence of all our industry and commerce, civilization and culture, on God in Nature, or at the beginning of the holiday season to be advised to seek the healing and heartening ministries of the hills and the sea-shore ; at all seasons God as the Creator as well as the Saviour should be gratefully and adoringly remembered.

(*b*) Although God has made man a little lower than the angels, and has crowned him with glory and honour, and has put all things in subjection to him (Psalm viii)—an estimate which modern science does not discredit—yet man is too prone to think of this vast, wonderful Universe as existing only to minister to his needs. An instance, which to the reflective mind will appear even ludicrous, of this self-centred view are the familiar lines of the poet :

" Full many a flower is born to blush unseen,
And waste its sweetness on the desert air."

as if all the beauty and fragrance in nature were intended only for the eye and the nose of man, and did not fulfil a vital function. Nature itself is so vast and wonderful, so beautiful and melodious, apart altogether from the supply of human needs, that for what God has made it, and is making it, we may adore Him, and should seek through it to approach Him. Modern society is becoming urbanized ; the achievements of man are so prominent in our civilization and culture, that there is distinct loss, religious and moral as well as physical. If modern man lived nearer nature, he might get closer to God ; for it is not the husbandman, the fisherman, or the shepherd who is inclined to atheism, but the man who lives the artificial life of modern society in the city. It is the duty of the preacher to his age to counteract this tendency to urbanization as it affects religion by giving a large place in his preaching to God's revelation of His power, wisdom, and goodness in nature.

(*c*) Modern science is not a hindrance, but can be a help in the discharge of this duty. As has already been indicated, it does certainly alter the conception of God, and His relations to the world, but that change is not loss but gain. The old form of the argument from design, in which the divine intention in a phenomenon was substituted for the natural explanation is certainly discredited. But it does present to us on a far vaster scale a universal order ; it shows to us everywhere in plant and animal life adaptations of the parts to the whole, and of the whole organism to its environment, which must fill us with wonder and must convince that in wisdom God is making all. Such a book as Dr. Simpson's *The Spiritual Interpretation of Nature* shows us that science does not banish God from the world He has made. It would be a mistake for a preacher to use many illustrations from science, as very often the illustration would need so long and difficult explanation, that instead of helping the hearers to understand it would hinder. Still less would any preacher commit himself to the kind of argument worked out in a once very popular book, *Natural Law in the Spiritual World*, which contains false analogies between the natural order and the spiritual life.

(*d*) In opposition to the conception of nature popularized by Tennyson's phrase, " red in tooth and claw," and the common misconception of the phrase " the struggle for existence," both of which give the impression that the animal world is a constant battle-field, the preacher should adduce the facts of co-operation as in the bee-hive, the ant-heap, the beaver-dam, the herd of wild cattle or horses, animal motherhood, and the nest as a home. He must not pretend that there are not in nature still problems for our thought, challenges for our faith in the goodness of God as Creator, in para-sitism, and the predatory instincts and habits of many animal species ; but it does seem very necessary to-day that he should offer all the con-siderations in relief of doubt that a widely spread false impression about the facts produces. If the psalmists could find a revelation of God in nature, much more should we to whom science has dis-closed so many of its secrets and displayed so many of its wonders. The preoccupation of man with himself, even with his duty and his destiny, is a narrowing and impoverishing of his manhood. He will surely enter into a closer communion with God, as he shares in understanding and appreciation the universal interest and activity of God. He should know and love nature because it is the Heavenly Father's handiwork ; he should accept as truth and duty what Coleridge teaches in the *Rime of the Ancient Mariner* :

" He prayeth well, who loveth well
  Both man and bird and beast.
He prayeth best who loveth best
  All things both great and small ;
For the dear God Who loveth us,
  He made and loveth all."

Would not this wider standpoint rebuke and correct the errors and wrongs of so much that must offend any sensitive soul in the civilization of to-day? Could we wantonly deface nature as we do, bringing ugliness where there was beauty; could we be as shamefully cruel as we are to what we are pleased to call the lower animals, not to meet our physical necessities but for the amusement of the idle rich, if we saw God in all, and through all, and over all? The old tale about the beginnings of the race has still its significance; God placed man in a garden "to dress it and to keep it" (Genesis ii. 15), and he has made the garden a wilderness, and despoiled it. God has given man "dominion over the works of His hands" (Psalm viii), but surely not that he might injure and destroy. As regards man God is Saviour, but even in the processes of nature and the activities of life we may with an observing eye and a discerning mind find tokens of "plenteous redemption" (Psalm cxxx. 7). That so many thoughtful and earnest people to-day are estranged from the Church is a challenge to its preachers. Have they made their message wide as are the activities of God in nature as well as history; is their method as varied as are the interests and tastes of men? Beauty, Truth, Holiness, and Love are all ways of God's approach to man, and man's return to God.

II. Even in Ancient Greece we have the beginnings of three of the sciences of mind—logic, ethics, and æsthetics—concerned with the law of reasoning, morality, and art, but for many centuries it was assumed that science could deal only with nature, and that all which concerned man fell to philosophy. It is now recognized, however, that mental processes can be investigated by the methods of science, with just such differences as the difference of the subject imposes.

(1) The science of psychology has at the present time a wider influence on popular thought and life than any other branch of human knowledge; and it is affecting both morality and religion so seriously that it is quite impossible for the Christian preacher to ignore it. It is true that in the literature which deals with human character and conduct there is an implicit psychology; the man of genius has keener sensibility and finer discernment, and so penetrates more deeply into the secrets of the soul. Contact with his fellow-men, as well as the study of human life as interpreted in literature, does greatly help the preacher in his task; but the exact observation and the accurate explanation of the mental processes, and the personal development which psychology offers do add much that is of great value. For it is imperatively necessary that the preacher like every other person seeking to instruct and influence others should know not only what he preaches but also those to whom he preaches, so that he may discover how to deliver his message most effectively, " to put it over " (as the Americans say) from his own to other minds. This is being generally insisted on in regard to teaching but it applies no less to preaching. So much preaching fails to effect all it might because the preacher lacks knowledge and judgment regarding the handling of his hearers. The stress

which is being laid on religious experience as confirming the truth of doctrine enhances the importance of psychology. The Bible as the literature of religious experience, through which God reveals Himself, is being more freshly and interestingly interpreted from this psychological standpoint. The inspiration of prophets and apostles is not now dogmatically defined as it once was ; the mental processes in man, in which the presence and activity of God by His Spirit are realized, are being closely studied with most fruitful results as regards our understanding. It is not regarded as irreverent even to try and gain some insight into the consciousness of Jesus as Son of God by such a study of His " inner life." The apostle Paul is a conspicuous instance of the development of the Christian personality ; and we can make his life in Christ far more intelligible to ourselves by the use of the same methods. In apprehending and appreciating what he preaches even the preacher is greatly aided by an adequate (and not superficial) knowledge of psychology. In the same way must he relate himself by intimate understanding with the religious experience and moral character of those to whom he preaches. He must make sure that the minds to which he addresses himself can assimilate the truth which he presents to them, and that assimilation depends not only on the capacity, but also on the content of the mind. The expression of the truth is relative to the mind of the preacher, but the impression made by the truth is relative to the mind of the hearers. In the processes of passing from mind to mind truth may be transformed into error. On these two grounds we may insist that a knowledge of psychology belongs to the necessary equipment of the ordinary preacher ; the genius may intuitively perceive what most men must by study acquire.

(2) It is not necessary to enter into fuller details regarding what may be called general psychology. There are some recent developments, claiming the name "the new psychology" which demand very much closer attention, for they are already affecting and are likely still more in the future to affect, the minds of the hearers, and that in many cases very injuriously. The preacher need not use the jargon which this science affects, but he must recognize, and guard his hearers against, two dangers from this quarter.

(a) *First of all* the prominence that is being given to the instincts, part of man's inheritance from his animal ancestry, and the subordination to these of reason and conscience, will tend to weaken the sense of moral responsibility. Man is sometimes represented as driven so hard by these instincts that reason or conscience seems impotent to check the downward career. This is not the place to discuss whether these impulses or appetites are properly called instincts ; so great a man of science as Dr. J. Arthur Thomson deprecates this loose use of the term, and maintains that man has few instincts as reason predominates in his life. What the preacher must contend against is the assumption that man is the slave of self, or sex, or herd instinct, and that reason's function is only to find plausible excuses for shameful indulgences. It is only because the resemblance of man and beast is exaggerated, and the difference between man and beast is ignored that such a degradation of human nature becomes possible. Without challenging the proved facts of human evolution, the preacher may with Wallace, the co-discoverer with Darwin of the theory of organic evolution by the survival of the fittest in the struggle of existence, assert the distance between man and beast which the progress of mankind mentally, morally, socially and spiritually proves to have been involved in the creation of man. Even Huxley recognized another law in man's social progress than in cosmic evolution. Man's self-consciousness of freedom and duty in morality, and of affinity and community with God in religion, is the ultimate court of appeal against an estimate of man which appears plausible only when what is distinctive of man is ignored. A first step towards securing faith in God may be to persuade men influenced by this " new psychology " that man is not only a little more cunning than the brute, but that he stands as the consummation of the evolution, its interpreter and completion. No message is more needed as the portal of the temple into which religion leads than insistence on the duty of " self-knowledge, self-reverence, self-control." Man must be made to believe in man if he is to exercise faith in God.

(*b*) When to this doctrine of the dominance of instinct is added the doctrine of man's subjection to the complexes in the region of the unconscious, making him the slave and the sport of he knows not what, from which deliverance can be found only by psycho-analysis, it is evident that ears are deafened for the appeal of the Gospel. For if man's moral life cannot be directed by conscience and controlled by will, but is the result of the dominance of instincts and the formation of complexes, morality and religion become a futile play on the surface of a life in bondage to lower forces. There are pathological cases that need and get benefit from this psycho-therapy ; but it would be absurd, if it were not so dangerous, to generalize from these abnormal cases, and treat all men as morally irresponsible. What the preacher should learn, however, is not to make hasty generalizations himself, and to assume that all men are equally normal, and all, therefore, have full responsibility. He must learn to discriminate, and to show compassion where compassion is needed and condemnation is not deserved. It is significant that to deal with these sub-conscious complexes it is necessary by the method of psycho-analysis to bring up the complex into consciousness, and to deal with it there. It is admitted by some psycho-analysts that suggestion (auto or hetero) is reinforced by faith in God. Prayer is a healing agency. Thus the subjective value of the moral resolve and the religious conviction may be admitted even from the standpoint of the new psychology.

(3) The qualifying word *subjective* in the pre-

ceding statement calls attention to another danger to religion which psychology may bring. It is the assumption that because psychology can describe the mental processes of faith, prayer, conviction and conversion, no objective reality is needed to explain the religious experience. The idea of God may be treated as a projection of the mind of man, to which nothing real corresponds. The help and comfort that the believer has found in prayer may be represented as auto-suggestion, and not at all a gift of God. In making any such assumption psychology is trespassing beyond its own proper field, for the problem of reality is one that belongs to metaphysics, and cannot be solved by any of the methods of a science. This subjectivism would involve the denial of the existence of an external world, as well as of God. With these problems the preacher is not called to deal in the pulpit directly ; but he must recognize that such an assumption may be in the minds of some of his hearers, and may make his arguments unconvincing and his appeals ineffective. What in this situation can he do ? He should deal often with what faith in God has been in Christian experience and done for Christian character ; and his own personality must give weight to his utterance. His certainty of faith, which loud declamation will not convey, but only a pervading persuasiveness in all his speech, will inspire confidence in others to make the venture of faith, so as to find the same verification in experience and character. A man must himself be very sure of God if he is to help others to become sure. Spiritual things are spiritually discerned ; and it is only as the worship of the Church, of which the preaching must be regarded as an integral part, is pervaded by the Spirit of God Himself, that men will be convinced of the present reality of God.

III. The modern thought with which the preacher must be familiar, in order that he may find the points of closest contact with his hearers, and so carry his message along the lines of least resistance, is not exhausted in modern science, physical, biological, or mental. There are current philosophies, more or less hostile to the Christian Gospel, and modes of thinking which are scarcely coherent enough even to be dignified as philosophies. The agnostic attitude is less prevalent than it was a generation ago ; the recent researches and speculations of science make the crude materialism of last century incredible. The practical needs as well as the intellectual questions of men are compelling them to reach out beyond the sensuous to the supersensible. It is true that, if in regard to the ultimate problems they have ceased to say *Matter*, many have not yet learned to say *God*.

(1) Christian Science is an attempt to deal with the problem of pain, and Spiritualism with the problem of death, and the number of their votaries is increasing rapidly, so rapidly that in not a few churches there is an appreciable loss of membership. The Christian preacher cannot simply ignore these influences. It is not enough to denounce them as *non-* or even *anti-*Christian. It is necessary to

recognize the human needs which find in them a satisfaction, and to present the Gospel as more adequately and permanently satisfying these needs ; and also at the very outset to acknowledge what measure of truth there is in them.

(i) As has already been indicated we must acknowledge the great extent to which the mind affects the body, the measure in which the health of the one depends on the happiness of the other. That pain may in many cases be relieved, and even removed, by calmness of spirit cannot be denied. The *mens sana* makes the *corpus sanum*. Again, there are many obscure psychical phenomena of which the mind in its normal activities is not aware ; we must not deprecate the thorough examination of these by science, although most of what claims to be science in this connection can hardly deserve the name. Religion must not set itself in opposition to any enquiry pursued in the interests of truth. As in seeking his father's asses Saul found a kingdom, so in Christian Science and Spiritualism the mind of man may come to know itself better, and gain more mastery over itself as well as over its body. Christian Science is a protest against the notion which religion has sometimes tended to encourage that God wills human sufferings. There are evil consequences that man brings upon himself by his own conduct, even when he does not know that he is doing wrong, and the pain is an indication of the wrongness, and so serves as a salutary discipline. There are evils which in ignorance, or indifference, or perversity, men inflict upon one another ; and these injuries too are fitted to quicken conscience and elicit the sense of responsibility. Nature too brings suffering ; but man may escape its dangers by knowledge of its laws and control of its forces. Man's development has been not hindered, but advanced by his struggle with nature. The finest qualities of human nature, sympathy, service and sacrifice have been evoked by the challenge of pain. It is thus that the Spirit of God in man reacts to the pain to which he is subject, and thus its evil can be turned to good. It is probable that some pain is inevitable in a finite creation which does not share the perfection of its Creator. It is certain that men inflict on themselves and one another far more pain than there need be. The preacher should not lend any countenance to the too common assumption that the beneficence of God's providence may be ignored, and only what hurts and grieves man is to be resignedly assigned to His will. The ever blessed God wills the good of all His children, and, when pain comes, He can by His grace enable them to rise above happiness to blessedness (as Carlyle has said),* and of that George Eliot has written: "We can tell it only from pain by its being what we would choose before everything else, because our souls see it is good."† Goethe's description of Christianity as the Sanctuary of Sorrow is

* " There is in man a higher than love of happiness, he can do without happiness and instead thereof find blessedness."— Sartor Resartus.

† *Romola* : Epilogue.

misleading ; it is a sanctuary in which sorrow can be transmuted into joy, and trial ends in triumph. The preacher needs not only the consolatory tone, which enables sufferers to endure, but the cheerful and courageous tone which inspires them to rejoice even in the afflictions which are but for a moment.

(ii) The last phrase of Paul's suggests that the preacher cannot deal with the problem of pain unless he puts in the forefront the Christian solution of the problem of death. The charge of "other-worldliness" which was brought against a former generation could not be brought for many years past when men were glorying in the material triumphs of modern civilization, or were pre-occupied by the need of social reform, so as to remove from that civilization such disadvantages and injuries as it had brought with it. For many the Kingdom of God had become no more than a present, progressive reality. The Christian hope was not preached with the certainty which inspires confidence. The denial of eternal punishment meant for many a diversion of interest from the future life altogether. The death of so many young and middle-aged men in the freshness and fulness of their manhood during the Great War, however, revived the longing for assurance that death does not end all. Even where the Christian hope was preached, its attachment to the present life of faith in Christ as Saviour and Lord was not so persuasively present as to lead by way of faith to hope. The discernment of spiritual values was too feeble ; the habit of relying on sensible evidence of reality was too strong ; and accordingly the appeal of the Gospel has seemed to many far less convincing than such physical evidence of the survival after death as spiritualism professes to be able to give. If the Christian hope is to be re-captured, faith must be restored as the discernment of the reality of the spiritual life. Mere survival, or survival under conditions similar to those of the present life, which seems to be all that spiritualism can offer, falls far short of what the Christian hope holds out. Life with Christ in growing likeness to Christ is the fulfilment of the promise of the life in Christ ; and the certainty of that fulfilment depends on spiritual discernment of the absolute value of the life of faith in Christ. It is only when for the believer " to live is Christ," that " to die is gain " (Phil. i. 21). This emphasis will remove the reproach of *other-worldliness* from the Christian hope, and ward off the danger of *this-worldliness* ; for it will ever present a life of such value for the whole human personality as to raise it above the contrast. This life will not be depreciated in comparison to that life, as each temporal occasion subserves the eternal destiny. The believer acts in time not for any fleeting interests, but for abiding values. He need not be less concerned about, or less active in making life here for others healthier, happier, and better because he himself has already a foretaste of " the inheritance of the saints in light." His own progress in Christian character will be not less, but more an object of aspiration and endeavour, because he is certain that its pertecting is assured. That the emphasis should be shifted from heaven as the reward of virtue or hell as the penalty of sin to an appreciation of the value of the Christian life here and now as the assurance of its continuance hereafter is not a matter for regret at all for the preacher as it cleanses and hallows the nature of his appeal.

(2) Two other tendencies may be grouped together, the Theosophical and the Ethical Society. Without entering into any details we may describe theosophy as an attempt to discover and express a human *wisdom* about God, assumed to be the common element of all religions, especially Hinduism and Christianity. What the Ethical Society aims at is a morality which seeks no sanctions from religion. Both are necessarily anti-Christian. in so far as Christianity claims the faith of man for Jesus Christ as the Son of God and the Saviour and Lord of mankind.

(i) " Theosophy," says one of its adherents, " is the body of truths which forms the basis of all religions, and which cannot be claimed as the exclusive possession of any. It offers a philosophy which renders life intelligible, and which demonstrates the justice and the love which guide evolution. It puts death in its rightful place as a recurring incident in an endless life, opening the gateway of a fuller and more radiant existence. It restores to the world the Science of the Spirit, teaching man to know the spirit as himself and the mind and body as his servants. It illumines the Scriptures and the doctrines of religions by unveiling their hidden meanings, and thus justifying them at the bar of intelligence as they are ever justified in the eyes of intuition."*

Without turning aside from our present purpose to consider whether its performances equal its pretensions, we may dwell on the significance of two of its features for the Christian preacher. What theosophy objects to in Christianity is its exclusiveness, and its appeal to authority. In all religions and not one only it professes to be able by *human wisdom*, and not *divine revelation*, to solve the problem of divine reality and human destiny. The duty that this challenge lays upon the preacher is twofold.

(*a*) Let him show his appreciation of the value of the other religions of the world, as not merely a vain human search after God, but as a real approach of man to God, who is really found by those who sincerely seek Him, however imperfect their conceptions of His nature, character, and purpose may be. But let him also show that the way of progress for mankind is not the eclecticism which tries to make a religion out of fragments of other religions, but by an expanding interpretation of Christianity as the one universal religion, in which all that is true and worthy in other religions may be taken up as the fulfilment of their prom se. I am quite certain that if interest is to be mainta ned in foreign missions the challenge which the other religions offer to the exclusiveness of the claim of Christ must be met, not by a depreciation of all

* Quoted *Encyclopædia of Religion and Ethics*, Vol. XII, p. 304.

others, but by a demonstration of the comprehensiveness of Christ Himself as " the desire of all nations." If this is not done, theosophy can charge Christianity with intolerance, and commend its own wider charity ; and that is a kind of appeal to which many to-day respond.

(b) Again, there is far more interest in the problems which the world and life offer than preachers often assume. There are Christian people who accept faith as a substitute for thought, and who are sometimes very vocal in their demand for the simple Gospel ; and the preacher may be tempted to win popularity by yielding to that demand, and giving his hearers only the milk for the babes. By all means let the preacher make his preaching simple by clear thought and plain speech ; and let him avoid as a plague all pedantry in the pulpit. That does not mean, however, that he must never deal with " the deep things of God." He must show that in the divine *Logos* (Word) are hidden all the treasures of human *Sophia* (Wisdom). His appeal must not be to an authority of Bible or Church which disregards or defies human intelligence, but to reason and conscience. He must commend his comprehensive message by convincing argument and persuasive appeal. One of the tragedies of the present hour is the extent to which the pulpit has lost command over the cultured class as well as the labouring masses. The show of a tolerant wisdom which theosophy makes challenges the Church to display the substance.

(ii) The claim of the Ethical Societies to formulate a morality which is independent of religious *sanctions* shows how superficial is the view of the relation of morality and religion ; and for this it must be admitted popular Christianity is in large measure responsible. To be good in the hope of heaven, and not to be bad from fear of hell—that is the connection for many persons between faith and works. As has already been indicated this is a phase of thought which is passing away, except in the ecclesiastical regiments that are always engaged in rear-guard actions in defence of positions which should be abandoned. What, however, seems still to be necessary to meet this challenge that morality is the gainer, and not the loser, by separation from religion is to show, as can be shown, that morality needs the roots of religion in the divine reality, and religion needs the fruits of morality in the human sphere. Comte recognized that his Positive Polity needed a basis in religion, and so he devised the religion of Humanity. The preacher may fully recognize what is true in these ethical movements ; that science may be a guide in morality and that the love of man may be its motive. Christianity does not give a complete code of morals applicable to all occasions ; but it lays down one general principle, common to religion and morality, that of love, and it gives content to that principle by instances of its application, such as forgiveness of injuries, the rendering of services, even when these involve self-sacrifice ; but above all its moral—" truth is embodied in a tale, a creed of creeds *wrought* in loveliness of perfect deeds." The application in detail of the principle and its instances in the varying circumstances of human society demands human prudence as well as divine wisdom, and as accurate and extensive a knowledge of the situation, physical, economic and social, as science can offer in each of these provinces. Christianity does not enjoin the doing of human duty solely as obedience to divine command, but as the living fruits of love to man. But for that love it finds a more constraining motive than natural affection, or the valuation of man merely as man, in the love of God in Christ inspiring both grateful love to God and generous love to man, and in the higher valuation of man as the child of God, beloved by God, and, therefore, to be loved by all who love God. Christianity thus affords morality a deeper motive and also a wider range, since God as well as man comes into its regard. In its enhancement of the value of man it gives morality a higher claim ; in its recognition of the relation of man to God it enlarges the moral sphere beyond the bounds of human society. The temporal evolution of morals is based on the eternal purpose of God. Further, if man be an immortal child of God, the pursuit of perfection does not become a quest, cut short by death, but a struggle assured of final victory. The faith in God also gives the assurance that man in his morality is not making a venture contrary to the nature of reality in a Universe which has no moral meaning ; but that the world's movement reaches the consciousness of its aim and

178

goal in the moral life of man. Morality in this vital relation to religion should have a large place in the pulpit, which should never lay itself bare to the charge of moral indifference ; and in showing how much religion can do for morality, the preacher must beware of belittling even the morality which has not yet found enlargement in religion. For in every Christian congregation there are men making the Christian profession who treat faith as a substitute, and not as a source of good works ; and they must never be given an excuse for their inconstancy in the Gospel which they hear. On the other hand there are many outside of the Christian Church who might be drawn into it if there were presented to them the Christian ideal, motive, power, and promise of morality as Christlike life because life in Christ.

(3) As the number of writings upon the subject shows, mysticism is very attractive to many minds. The difficulty of dealing with this subject is the ambiguity of the term. It may mean that immediate contact of the soul with God which must be the inmost shrine of all religion, that intimate communion with God in Christ which Paul knew, and for which all Christians should aspire, that direct action of the Spirit of God in the inner life of man which is the condition of discernment and sanctity. In this sense Christianity is essentially mystical ; this is the distinctive Christian experience, although there are many Christians who do not attain it. It needs to be insisted on against dogmatism, ritualism, or legalism, all religion as

we may call it at second hand. But the term may also mean the approach to God by an artificial process in abnormal psychic conditions with visions and voices. It is not necessary so to seek God ; and in these ways He is not necessarily found. In the literature of mysticism there has been a tendency to enhance the importance of these experiences ; and many are attracted to them by their strangeness rather than their worth. A man may be a saint without them ; and a man may fail to become a saint who has them. Against the tendency to isolate the distinctive Christian experience from the general personal activity, the preacher needs to lay stress on Christ in His historical mediation as the true and living way to God, on faith, love, and hope as the exercises by which God in Christ can be possessed, and on the Christian life in the world as the surest proof of " the life hid with Christ in God." Nevertheless the preacher will disappoint some of the finest spirits among his hearers if he is doctrinal and practical, but gives them no sense of the nearness of the divine Presence, or the sureness of the working of the Spirit of God, even as the Gospel is preached. If Christ Himself is not made real as the words are spoken about His truth and grace, the souls that hunger and thirst after God will miss the Bread from Heaven and the Water of Life, of which Christian preaching should be the channel.

(4) Touching now on some of the philosophies of the hour, (i) there is an idealism and optimism, which sometimes claims to be Christian, that ignores

on the one hand the reality of sin and on the other the necessity for grace. That we cannot now preach the doctrine of original sin, and of total depravity, does not justify the superficial moral estimate which does not take seriously the actual sins of men, and the evils that are deep-rooted in human society. To think so lightly of sin as to take God's forgiveness as a matter of course is to miss that understanding of the grace of God which excites wonder, adoration, and gratitude. The Fatherhood, which is good-nature, tolerant of wrong-doing, is not the revelation of the Son of God, which came and could not but come through the redemption of man in His sacrifice for sin. This impoverishment and enfeebling of the Gospel sometimes arrogates the title of *theological liberalism*. It must be met not by a reaction to old phrases, which can be condemned as obscurantism ; but only by the evangelicalism which presents the operation both of sin and grace in the terms of our modern knowledge of man, and especially of the moral and religious life. Such knowledge does not make sin less real, or grace less necessary.

(ii) There is current to-day a *pragmatism*, which tells us that *that is truth which works*. If the practical effects of a belief are good it is argued it may be held as true ; and its truth need not be tested in any other way.

(*a*) Now human history offers many instances of a superstition which has led men and women to be devout, and to do their duty ; but the discovery that it was error has robbed it of its practical efficacy.

As Christianity is truth both objectively and subjectively, it must seek certainty regarding the object of faith and sincerity in the quality of the faith ; and it must oppose itself to any falsity. Because readers of the Bible have derived profit from an arbitrary method of its interpretation, some hearers resent the candour of the preacher who sets forth the only accurate method. Even if the text " Almost thou persuadest me to be a Christian " (Acts xxvi. 28) has been a means of blessing to many, it remains a mistranslation, and the honest preacher cannot use it. Because the doctrine of eternal punishment has frightened some sinners into repentance, its truth cannot be assumed, if it can be proved to contradict the conception of God as Father which Christ has given. Even to the preacher who knows nothing about pragmatism as a philosophy, a practical pragmatism may become a temptation. The tempter says : " Do not contradict the error that comforts some believers ; do not proclaim the truth that might disturb some saints." Apart altogether from the absolute claim of truthfulness, the preacher should think of the disastrous reaction on his influence when the lack of candour is discovered. While there must be consideration, tact, and wisdom in exposing error and declaring truth, the preacher must hold it as a sacred duty to search for truth, based on evidence and reason, as that which alone can permanently and universally work. Probably nothing has done more to lessen the influence of the pulpit than the assumption for which some preachers afford a justification, that many preachers, even when not deliberately uncandid, do not allow themselves to think lest they should lose their working hypothesis, and be less practically effective because less intellectually certain. After I had given a lecture on Revelation and Inspiration from the modern standpoint, several of my hearers confessed that they could not leave the old paths and venture on the new, as they did not know where they might be led. One does not want to judge timid souls harshly, but does not that attitude betray a singular distrust of the guidance of the sincere thinker by the Spirit of truth into all the truth ?

(*b*) The philosophy of pragmatism is really an agnosticism in disguise ; it disbelieves the possibility of man attaining a truth which, in its self-evidence apart from its practical effects, will satisfy the mind ; and therefore it bids men stop their quest when satisfied with these practical effects. I have never been able to take pragmatism as anything but a " freak " philosophy ; and James, its most brilliant exponent, as engaged in the game of " pulling the leg " of a too credulous public, a public glad to be relieved of the hard labour of thinking. To religion especially does such a philosophy seem fatal. For religion is the quest of ultimate cause, final purpose, and essential reality ; and sincerely pursued it is rewarded with certainty, with the substance and not the shadow. The Christian preacher, if he possesses the certainty, must pass it on if his hearers are to find the satisfaction of mind which they rightly seek.

All that pragmatism may teach the preacher is not to preach what has only intellectual interest, but no practical effect, if such truth there be, and to reinforce his proof of the truth of doctrine by showing what are its practical effects, if it is believed.

It is impossible to give an exhaustive description of the various phases of modern thought with which the Christian preacher, if he is to adapt his message to his intellectual environment, must make his account. As will be shown in a later chapter, the Gospel is the preacher's message, and nothing here said is intended even to suggest that the pulpit is to be made a platform from which the varied and varying 'isms of the day are to be expounded to the " ears itching to hear some new thing." All that this survey, incomplete as it is, is intended to do is to show that the preacher must be familiar with what his hearers are thinking, if he is to get his Gospel home. If a preacher has a congregation which is unreached by any of these movements, he need not, to gratify his own intellectual interests, concern himself with them in his pulpit, but in his study it is well for him to be always widening his own intellectual outlook. The preacher must not, however, too readily assume such isolation of all his hearers. As one who gives lectures, followed by questions, on theological and ethical subjects, I am often surprised to find how wide-spread bewilderment of mind is, and how much certainty is desired. Questions of faith and morals are being discussed in newspapers, novels, and plays ; many religious " fads " are being spread by a zealous propaganda. Even if the majority of a congregation is content with traditional and conventional preaching, there is sure to be in most places a minority, even if small, with a questioning mind and a bewildered conscience, which is looking for counsel and help, and, if disappointed, may be estranged not only from the Church, but even from Christ. Better it is sometimes to disappoint a large number by giving them something of which they feel no need than to be always disappointing a few, or even one only, by withholding what is craved. The lost sheep whom the shepherd should seek may not be a sinner but a doubter or an enquirer ; there is an intellectual as well as a moral or religious tending of the flock.

CHAPTER III

THE PREACHER AND MODERN SOCIETY

I. THE title of this chapter is itself an indication of a characteristic feature of our own time. During the greater part of last century the conception of the preacher's task was *individualist*. It was individual experience and individual character about which preaching concerned itself, and if any social reference appeared at all, it was as individual influence on others. To-day we are learning a great deal about the Social Gospel, the relation of the Church to Society.*

(1) The reason for the change is to be found in circumstances and in opinions and sentiments. The outward conditions have affected the inward. Men are thinking and feeling differently because their world is different. When we condemn theories of the past about human society as inadequate we often forget they were as adequate to the existing society as ours are likely to be. The fact acts on the thought, and the thought reacts on the fact; and there is a constant interaction of mind and world. When social relations were very much more simple

* See *A Guide to Preachers*, Fourth Section, pp. 325-343, for a discussion of *How to meet the Age* in its social problems.

186

than they are to-day, as in the eighteenth century, the mechanical theory of society as a sum of separate units artificially held together (as by an assumed social contract) was not so remote from reality as it would appear to-day, although there can be no doubt that the forms of social theory were also affected by the dominance of physics in science. After the Industrial Revolution, when social relations became much more complex because of increasing economic interdependence, as in the nineteenth century, the organic conception emerged, in which we have also to recognize the influence of the prevalent biological interest. Herbert Spencer, it is to be observed, in working out this biological analogy confines himself to the external features of society, and does not extend it to the personal relations of human beings; indeed he repudiates any such extension on the ground that pleasure or pain is, and cannot but be, individual. Advancing in his theory beyond individualism, he adheres to it in practice. By pressing the analogy beyond its proper application, he finds a justification for the policy of *laissez-faire*. The wrongs, losses, and miseries which resulted from the survival of this policy in an era in which, to use Lord Beaconsfield's words about Protection, it should have been both *dead* and *damned*, stimulated in men of more advanced mind the social consciousness, a realization that the economic interdependence involves, and ought to involve a great deal more than Spencer allowed, and that as there is a personal interdependence, moral obligation goes far beyond the bounds set by individualism. Society is not only economically organic, but through the whole range of human activities. There is not only an external unity; there is an internal consciousness of unity. There may not be a common consciousness in a society, but there is a community of interests among the members of a society. *Community* is the term that is displacing the term *organism* as a more adequate category for human society.* May we not here also recognize the influence of psychology, the science to which increasing attention is being given ? The current view of society is thus affected on the one hand by the actual state, and on the other by the dominant conceptions of science. How does this development affect the Christian preacher in the presentation of his message ?

(2) He should have no hesitation in welcoming it; because all these theories are anticipated in Paul's thought about the Church, the mechanical in his metaphor of the temple (Eph. ii. 20, 21), the organic in his analogy with the body (1 Cor. xii. 12-31), the community in his assertion of what Spencer ignores, that "whether one member suffereth, all the members suffer with it; or one member is honoured, all the members rejoice with it" (v. 26), and that community is not merely a convergence of human individuals, it has its source in the common possession (Koinonia, community) of the Holy Ghost (2 Cor. xiii. 14). The Church so conceived is the ideal, to which human society, when truly Christian, should

* See *Community : a Sociological Study,* by McIver.

conform, and also the agency for the realization of the ideal.

II. The preacher need not hesitate about abandoning individualism, and accepting this conception of the interdependence of individuals in the community of society.

(1) This does not involve, however, that he should rush to the other extreme of collectivism. With that as an economic theory he has no immediate concern, as Christianity is not to be identified with any view about the possession of goods or the regulation of industry, except that it must insist on the application of the Christian standards of conduct in all human relations. Against collectivism as a tendency of thought he must be on his guard, for the Gospel asserts the value of the individual soul, and the responsibility and the liberty of each man. If the Christian preacher puts the main emphasis on economic conditions and social relations, and allows individual conduct and character to fall into the background, he is unfaithful to what is distinctive of the Gospel. The regeneration of individuals must be his primary concern, although he will give an inadequate conception of what that involves if he does not give an important, if subordinate, place to social amelioration, for there is this relation between the two.

(a) The environment of many men is such as to hinder improvement and foster degradation. While there may be, and have been, saints in slums, and there is much heroism and beauty of human character to be met with in mean streets, yet it is well-nigh a forlorn hope to improve the souls of many while their conditions all tend to the ruin of manhood. Social reform may prepare the way of the Lord in the evangelization of the masses. It is certain that a Church indifferent to the wrongs and miseries of the common people will not, and cannot, commend the Gospel to them.

(b) Again, what is the end of individual salvation ? Men are saved by Christ, not for safety hereafter, but for service here. However respectable morally and religiously a life may be, if it is selfish it cannot in a truly Christian sense be said to be saved. The man who is indifferent to the evils of his environment, and does nothing to relieve and remove them, is responsible for their continuance, and thus for the souls that are lost because enmeshed in these evils. The man on the contrary who has open eyes to discover, and ready hands to remove, these evils, is developing his own Christian character, is giving Christ the opportunity of making him by His Spirit what a Christian should be, who bears the likeness of the Son of Man who " came not to be ministered unto, but to minister, and to give his life a ransom for many " (Matt. xx. 28).

(2) It is often objected, however, that all a Christian needs to be and to do is to live according to the Christian standard in his individual relations, to cultivate in himself the Christian graces and virtues. This argument is much used by those who are opposed to the Social Gospel. Against it two things have to be said, one a review of the past, the other a forecast of the future.

(*a*) Under the kind of individualist preaching which prevailed in most pulpits during last century, an industrial system and a social order were allowed to develop, unchecked and unrelieved, which are a menace to all the higher interests of mankind. Some improvement in material conditions there has been; but there is an antagonism of economic interests, an estrangement of social classes, a spirit of revolt on the side of the masses, and of panic on the side of the classes that are manifestly contrary to the purpose of God for His human family.

(*b*) If the future is not to reproduce the evils of the past, there must be a discovery and treatment of the causes of the disease in the body politic, and not merely an attempt to relieve the superficial symptoms. The individual philanthropy which the Christian Church commended, and in some quarters still commends as the sole moral obligation to society is quite inadequate to remove the sources of these evils, and even to relieve the symptoms. Not palliatives of charity, but the drastic remedies of justice without prejudice or partiality are what the situation demands. A man cannot be his best, or do his most as a member of society by isolated effort; he must promote a corporate consciousness of the evils to be removed, a corporate conscience which will demand their removal, a corporate activity in removing them. There will still be need for individual philanthropy, as social reform will not speedily atone for the neglects of the past generations; but more and more must *social politics* displace *individual philanthropy* as the sole duty of the Christian. On a banner in a procession of unemployed a number of years ago there was "this strange device," "Curse your charity, Give us justice." It was crudely expressed, but it was a legitimate challenge of much of the moral teaching of the Church. The contrast may be also expressed this way. The teaching of Christian ethics must be less psychological and must become more sociological. Instead of a description of graces and virtues there must be a discussion of social institutions, what they are and how they ought to be, from the standpoint of the Christian ideal of the Kingdom of God.

III. It is certain that such preaching would not be popular, that it would in many congregations excite opposition.

(1) Many hearers are delighted to listen to eloquent descriptions of the Christian excellences *in vacuo* ; but they resent if the searching scrutiny of the preacher finds out the un-Christian practices and relations of their homes and businesses. A Christian should be willing to suffer an uneasy and even a wounded conscience; but there are many professors of the Christian faith who instead of setting about an amendment of their ways are angry with the man who has compelled them to recognize that there is need for amendment. If the preacher's message does not convict them of sin, and they can as before God claim " a conscience void of offence," they should be grateful to him for this occasion of self-satisfaction. If, however, they are convicted, should he be blamed ? Or should

they not blame themselves ? A Greek sage was told that the boys were laughing at his singing; he did not get angry, but answered, " Then I must learn to sing better." The extreme impatience and irritation that some hearers are displaying whenever the industrial system and the social order are brought into the light of the Gospel, and there in many of their features stand condemned, is surely an evidence of an uneasy conscience. The demand for the simple Gospel is, even if unconsciously, a desire to enjoy the benefits without accepting the obligations of Christ; it is a subtle form of the error that Paul condemned: " Shall we continue in sin that grace may abound ? " (Rom. vi. 1). When a Church attempts to silence the voice of Christ to the conscience it is committing suicide. It is not for the pew, even if it pays the piper, to call the tune. The preacher is responsible for his message to Christ, to the Gospel of His truth and grace, to the Church as His spiritual body, but not to the local congregation.

(2) The authority of the preacher imposes a responsibility. His manner and his method of presenting his message should be in harmony with the Spirit of the Gospel, compassionate, considerate, courteous, persuasive, and not domincatory and domineering. In most cases when a preacher gets into trouble with his hearers, it is because he lacks tact, or is ill-mannered. The preacher must qualify himself for the discharge of the difficult duty of applying the Christian ideal and motive to the whole of human life by adequate knowledge of his subject,

so that he may command respect for his competence, even if he should fail to secure agreement with his conclusions. About the personal obligations of the preacher there can be no doubt. But a very much more difficult question arises, as to what may be included, or what must be excluded, from the contents of the message. The problem is not solved by the formula that the preacher is concerned only with general principles, and he must leave to his hearers their particular application; for to adopt a distinction made by Kant, the principles without the applications are empty, and the applications without the principles are blind. An abstract statement has little or no force without a concrete illustration. To tell men to be just is not enough, for justice in a simple, undeveloped society means less in the duties it involves than in a complex, civilized community. To love mercy does not mean merely giving alms. To walk humbly with God will affect a man's attitude to his fellow-men as alike children of the same heavenly Father. Honesty does not include only payment of debts, but also consideration for others in making contracts. Who is able by his own individual conscience to determine all that equal love to self and neighbour involves? We assume far too instructed and sensitive a conscience in most Christian people, if we suppose that it can be a sure guide to conduct amid all the perplexities and difficulties of life in a society such as ours. For the security and progress of society it is not enough that each man should do right and avoid wrong according to his own judgment; what all men need is to be instructed as to what is right and wrong. The Master Teacher was not content with generalities; often he gives the illustration without stating the principle, and leaves His hearers to infer the principle from the illustration. So different are the circumstances of His age and ours, that His illustrations must not be treated as applications of the principles in all times. Instructions He gave His disciples do not at once give us sure guidance for the needs of each hour.

(3) The preacher must be thoroughly familiar with the principles of morality as taught by Jesus either in the general statement or the particular illustration. He must, however, know also his times and surroundings so as to be able to judge whether the concrete instance does or does not afford guidance, and to determine in what way the principle can be best illustrated for his hearers.

(a) It is well for him, however, to be acutely aware of the limitation of his knowledge and the fallibility of his judgment, so that he should not display either his ignorance or his arrogance. There is a multitude of details in every business of which only experience and practice can give the knowledge, and it is prudent for the preacher not to attempt to tell how the business is to be managed. There are economic solutions of the social problem which have their ardent advocates, who would like to capture the pulpit for their propaganda; but as has already been indicated, neither individualism nor collectivism can claim to be the distinctively Christian solutions to which the Church can commit itself, although individual Christians are entitled after adequate study to express their preferences. Paul's letter to Philemon is an example for the preacher. The apostle did not advocate the abolition of slavery, but he did require such a relation between master and slave as led to the abolition. There are defects in the relation of employer and employed to-day which the Christian conscience cannot hesitate in condemning; but it cannot be said that there is such a consensus of Christian judgment as would justify a condemnation of the relation as such. In a strike or a lock-out the Christian moral issue is seldom if ever so clear as would justify the preacher in taking sides. He may at such a time insist that economic considerations should always be subordinate to moral obligations; and that the mutual moral obligations must be determined by the common relation of all men to God as Father. The preacher is following in the steps of Jesus and Paul when he urges that employers and employed must treat one another as members of the one human family of God.

(*b*) Can he go beyond the common opinion of his congregation in more concrete applications of this principle? If he lacks practical experience of the details of any business, he has, or if he is properly equipped, he should have, a wider knowledge of ethics than the business man needs to acquire for the successful conduct of his business, a more intimate understanding of the Christian ideal and motive, a more instructed and sensitive conscience than in the conditions of industry and commerce a layman is likely to acquire, for it is not easy in the world as it now is, to keep " a conscience void of offence," and to escape becoming unwittingly conformed to the world's ways. How many a Christian man would condemn Jesus' teaching as impracticable if he were hearing it for the first time ! As a preacher who has had practical experience of business, I affirm with all deference to the laymen who are in business, that the properly trained preacher is likely to have a wider knowledge and a keener insight in regard to Christian morality, even in its particular applications except as regards expert knowledge of the details of any business. While the preacher cannot shirk his personal responsibility to give such guidance as he has qualified himself to give, and while one recognizes that progress has usually been first advocated by the solitary voice, and it would be a great loss were not some men ready to take the risks, and pay the price of pioneers; yet we seem now to have reached a stage in which there should be concerted action on the part of the Christian Church to assert the authority of Christ in every realm of human life and to show the application of His principles to, and the realization of His Spirit in all human interests and activities.

(c) The man must be exceptionally endowed with capacity or conceit who thinks himself competent to deal with all these problems alone. Books are not an adequate help, as they are limited by the individual knowledge and insight of their writers, even though the relevant literature is increasing and improving. What is necessary is that Christians should take counsel together to discover the mind of the Lord—men active in industry and commerce, or engaged in public service, experts in different sciences, preachers and leaders of the Churches. Time spent at conferences, if they are properly arranged and conducted, is not wasted for any preacher. These conferences must be held on a national scale, as was Copec in Birmingham, in April, 1924, or universal as the Conference on Christian Life and Work in Stockholm in 1925. In this matter we are but at the beginning of things. The Churches generally have to make up immense arrears of knowledge and judgment. The world is challenging the Church of Christ to discharge a task for which it is not yet competent; and yet it is a task that brooks no delay. Society is drifting away to shipwreck, unless Christ can be given command of the helm to steer its course amid all the threatening perils to security and progress. However reluctantly and modestly, the Christian preacher must already make the venture to offer to others such solutions as many of the best minds concerned with these problems have agreed upon. He may speak confidently where there is certainty of judgment; and he must speak diffidently where only conjecture can be made. He will often feel as did Augustine when writing on the doctrine of the Trinity, "we speak that we may not keep silence." But if, as in the Parable of the Last Judgment, Christ identifies Himself with the world's needs, is not the world's challenge also His call, and who, when He calls, dares disobey? Surely He will not send His servants to this warfare at their own charges; but He will Himself by His Spirit be " a mouth and wisdom " to the pulpit of to-day. If in this hour of visitation the Church will, in the words of Carey, " attempt great things for God," it may also "expect great things from God."

IV. General counsels, however, are often resented as disturbing ignorance but not imparting knowledge, and I feel, therefore, an obligation laid upon me to refer to some of the questions with which the preacher is called to deal—not to offer solutions of the problems, but to show how these may be dealt with in the pulpit.

(1) The first place must be given to the family, an institution which, if the preacher is guided by the teaching of Jesus, will be dealt with as of primary importance to social stability. While owing to the political situation of His time and people Jesus held aloof from public affairs, and offered no social programme, He was very emphatic and authoritative in what He said about marriage and parenthood. While there are notable examples of conjugal fidelity and parental or filial piety in the literature of paganism, from the early days of Christianity the Christian home was in striking contrast to the pagan. No one can doubt that the home is menaced to-day, and the Christian ideal of it more than ever needs reassertion.

(a) The entry of women into industry and their consequent political emancipation, good as they may be in themselves, have brought perils to the unity of the family. The legal recognition of conflicting interests of husband and wife, inevitable as it is, must affect the intimacy of the relation. The economic independence of the children lowers the authority of the parents at an age when guidance is most needed. At an enquiry, over which I presided, on the treatment of venereal disease by the community, several medical men complained that they had never heard a sermon on marriage and parenthood. The preacher need not involve himself in a discussion of the grounds on which divorce may be granted; but he should insist that the Christian ideal is an indissoluble, life-long companionship, even if he has to admit that the Christian standard cannot be legislatively imposed on those who have not accepted the yoke of Christian discipleship; but that, even in dealing with those persons, moral interests, and not personal considerations, should be held to be decisive of any modifications of the Christian principle. With this topic it will be necessary for him to deal but seldom, if at all.

(*b*) Although he may offend some extreme feminists he may insist that Christian motherhood is the finest career any woman could desire, and the greatest service she can render to the community. On the question that is being so frankly, and often so foolishly, discussed, the restriction of the family, there is no generally accepted Christian conviction which it is the duty of the preacher to assert; but two things, it seems to me after a study of the problem in all its aspects, the preacher can confidently say: first of all he should, in opposition to many of the advocates of restriction, assert that it must not be used as a substitute for the social reform which would improve the conditions of living for the toiling masses; not less life under bad conditions, but more life under good is the aim to be set. Secondly he should insist on the blessing of parenthood, even when that involves hardship and sacrifice. The cases where restriction by other means than the natural way may be legitimate, if such there are, are not a matter for public discussion, but for private consultation of the doctor and the minister. A home where there is poverty may be a genuinely Christian home, and a home where ease, comfort, and luxury abound may lose its Christian character.

(c) In the changed conditions it must be recognized that parental, especially paternal, authority cannot now be asserted in the old way, nor is it consistent with the Christian spirit that it should. Personal influence must take its place, and that influence cannot be assumed when the need for it arises; it must be already possessed, and it can be possessed only as the parents have been companions of their children from their earliest years. Men and women in public life are doing a grave injustice to their families if they are not finding time for such companionship; for the father no less than for the mother is this neglect a failure of duty to the community. In this connection there is, however, the danger of family selfishness; the children no less than the parents should feel themselves members of a society wider than the home. The affections and intimacies of the home, valuable in themselves, are enhanced as a preparation for the wider social obligations. These are but a few imperfect suggestions as to the way in which the preacher may discharge what I insist again must be regarded as a primary claim on his witness.

(2) The child passes from the home to the school. His education does not begin only then; it should have begun with the beginning of life. The mother is the most influential educator; and it will be difficult for the school to correct the errors of the home. Good habits can be taught, and bad inclinations restrained, from babyhood. And occasionally the preacher may well remind parents of their duty and privilege as educators. I need not now dwell on the importance of preaching itself being educative, as the guiding principle of this second part of this book is what and how to teach and consequently train from the pulpit.

(a) What in accordance with such a practice the preacher may assert as a theory is that religion and education should be inseparable. An education is not only incomplete, but perverse, which is not religious, and a religion is shallow and unstable which is not educative. If God be what religion professes that He is, the reality and the value for each man with which nothing else can compare, what kind of a personal development can that be, in which man's relation to Him is ignored or neglected? Or again, if religion be not a part of life, separable from other parts, but a quality of the whole personality, how can religion become all that it should be, unless it is made a constant influence in the whole personal development ? Without depreciating the value of what may be described as *revivalist evangelism* when sinners need to be turned from the error of their ways, if the methods are psychologically sound, we may claim that what is even more important is *educational evangelism*, the influence of the Gospel as pervasive, unostentatiously but all the more effectively, of the whole life. It cannot begin too early, and it need not stop with youth. For in recent years attention has very properly been called to the need of adult education, not less in religion and morals than in general knowledge.

(*b*) One of the lamentable results of what many people are hardening their hearts against acknowledging as our unhappy divisions is that the school has become the battleground of sectarianism. An education of youth, psychologically sound, need not contain any of the elements about which Churches dispute and divide. Instead of bringing the education controversy into the pulpit, let the pulpit, strive rather to bring a generous view and a gracious spirit into the school. It would be a pity if the pulpit however, confined its interest to what is generally regarded as distinctively religious education. Only a timid or cowardly obscurantism can fear knowledge or culture; an enlightened and confident faith can seek and find God in every human activity untainted by sin. That the preacher should help and encourage the Sunday School, and the Bible Class, and talk about their tasks and needs in the pulpit on fit occasion, such as the Sunday School Anniversary, or Young People's Day, goes without saying. What may need asserting with emphasis is that the preacher should advocate an ideal of an education, accessible to all according to their capacity, which will develop the whole man with all his talents, in all his relations to nature, society, and God, and not merely prepare him, as some are clamouring to-day it alone should, for his earthly calling or his duties as a citizen.

(3) To many it seems a foolhardy adventure for the preacher to follow the boy or girl into the sphere of industry. Some preachers even regard economics and politics as " taboo " for the pulpit. But if Christianity is concerned with the whole manhood of every man, and if where Christ comes He comes " to reign with undisputed sway " in the whole life, how can the Church be indifferent to, or silent about conditions which so potently affect not only the health and happiness, but even the morals and the religion of most men and women ? Not only so, have not the Hebrew prophets, beginning with Amos, taught us that God is righteous, and exacts righteousness in men, and that to do justly and to love mercy no less than to walk humbly with Him is God's requirement, and not the multitude of sacrifices ? The acceptableness of a people before God, I venture to say, depends much more on what is done in workshop, factory, shop, and market than what is said in church. There is the searching test and the convincing proof of the reality of the religion. Allusion has already bee

made in a previous section to the method of handling such questions in the pulpit, as here more than in any other sphere lies the greatest difficulty for the preacher, calling for the possession in a large measure of the cardinal virtues of wisdom, and courage that he may avoid alike foolish speech and cowardly silence. So dominant is the influence in modern society of economic conditions, however, that no preacher can suppose that he is meeting the challenge of the times unless he summons industry to appear before the judgment-bar of Christ.

(4) If there is objection to economics in the pulpit, the opposition to politics is often even more vehement; and discord is introduced into a congregation when the preacher deals with these topics.

(*a*) The fault for this discord may lie with the preacher; even if he is adequately informed, he may be partisan in spirit, and provocative in manner. But it may also lie with the congregation. Christian men are all the week being influenced in their political opinions by a party press, and get irritated when genuinely Christian principles are being expounded from the pulpit, which challenge their opinions. When a hearer's opinions are so challenged he need not assume that the preacher is wrong; it is better for him to enquire if his own opinions are right. I am not defending foolish, rash speech in the pulpit; but I am pleading for candid self-examination in the pew.

(*b*) When the State was concerned only with the protection of persons and property against force or fraud, and its functions had not been extended much beyond the bounds which *laissez-faire* theories would set to it, a plausible case could be made out for the silence of the pulpit on all that belongs to the wide realm of politics. Even then it might have been the duty of the pulpit to challenge these restrictions, and to assert that a community has wider obligations and heavier responsibilities than such a theory admits. The State to-day, however, is concerned with many matters with which the Church was formerly charged; education, the care of the poor, the protection of morals even have passed from the one to the other. Can the Church resign all interests in these matters ? Economic conditions to which it has been urged Christianity cannot be indifferent, are more and more being regulated by the State. Many business men, who object to what they are pleased to call its interference, when the action of the State is directed toward the protection of the working-classes, are quite clamorous for protection of their trade against foreign competition. It is not for self-interest, but for the common good to determine what the State may or may not do.

(*c*) In recent years we have realized how much the lives of men are affected by the policy of the State in international relations, how it is impossible to separate home and foreign politics. How enthusiastic was the support of many pulpits, unchallenged by the pews, to the Great War ! Whether, even if the support was justified, it was not more enthusiastic than it should have been is a question regarding which we may say " let the dead past bury its dead." Can anybody doubt that it is the duty of the pulpit to condemn war as an un-Christian method of settling disputes, to promote peace by an advocacy of Christian universalism, a love of all men in Christ which will rise above all differences of interest, class, nation, or colour ? If so, home no less than foreign politics must be brought under the scrutiny of the Christian conscience. A policy of national selfishness is provocative of war, because it stirs in other nations suspicions and enmities. The patriotism of the pulpit, therefore, must not be exclusive, but expansive, love of country but an intensified form of love of all mankind; for only thus can the Christian universalism be realized in international relations by the enthronement of the Prince of Peace.

CHAPTER IV

THE PREACHER AND THE GOSPEL

I. The preceding pages might leave on the reader an impression altogether different from what the writer desires. The conviction that inspires this volume is that the preacher's business is to preach the Gospel; and nothing that has been written about the Bible, Modern Thought, or Modern Society is intended to displace the Gospel from its central position, and its supreme authority.

(1) When the whole Bible is regarded as equally inspired, then there is the danger of the Gospel which it enshrines being so surrounded by and entangled in matters historical, doctrinal and practical, that it does not stand forth in its distinctive features, and men are compelled to ask in bewilderment: What is God's unique message to men ?* All literary and historical criticism of the Bible can serve to detach the heavenly treasure from the earthen vessel. For instance men who assign an equal authority to the Old and the New Testament, as believers in verbal inspiration must, cannot detach the conception of God as Father which Christ

* See *A Guide to Preachers*, Second Section, for an earlier attempt to show preachers *How to State the Gospel.*

208

as Son alone has given, or can give, from the very crude notions that at one stage of their religious development men were alone capable of receiving; similarly a representation of the death of Christ based on the ancient ideas of sacrifice would be offensive to a fully enlightened Christian conscience. Recognizing the intellectual interest of modern Biblical scholarship, I value it most of all for the possibility that it gives us of finding the Gospel in the Bible. Modern thought cannot offer us a substitute for the Gospel, an up-to-date equivalent for " Jesus Christ, the same yesterday, to-day, yea and for ever." What it can disclose to us are the present needs that the grace of Christ alone can meet, the present hindrances to the approach of enquiring minds to His truth, the present terms which will make His appeal most intelligible and credible. Modern Society, even if improved beyond the dreams of the most ardent reformer, cannot displace the Church of Christ as the home of cleansed and hallowed human life; but it is amid the difficulties and perplexities of present conditions that the Gospel can, if its principles are applied, prove itself the power and wisdom of God unto social salvation. It is to throw into bolder relief the distinctiveness of the Gospel, to show how fully it answers the questions of the mind, and how fitly it solves the problems of the life, that all the studies of the preacher, as discussed in the previous chapters, converge.

(2) A definition of the Gospel cannot be given, but a description of some of its features may be

attempted. The man who claims to put the Gospel in a nutshell offers a measure, not of the Gospel, but of his own mind. The clamour for a *simple* Gospel is a stupid and lazy demand. It is true that the Gospel can be so presented as to reach very simple minds; but what they can receive does not exhaust the content of the Gospel; for God's dealing in grace with the sin of man is wide as man's need, and rich as God's resources. It has pleased God that in Christ should dwell the fulness of the Godhead, and men may receive of that fulness, and grace on the top of grace. We must beware of using language that belittles the greatness of the Gospel.

(*a*) The Gospel has a double aspect, human and divine. It is the presentation of truth in human language, but in the presentation the reality, which is in the truth declared, is made present and active. The words of men could not convey grace and produce faith, were not God Himself in His Spirit fulfilling His own purpose through human agency. It is not belief in the doctrine of Christ and His Cross that saves, it is Christ Himself who is in faith received as Saviour. Paul's language about the Gospel would appear exaggerated, if he were thinking only of his own argument and appeal; it is Christ presented in the preaching of the Gospel and apprehended in the hearing who is the wisdom and the power of God unto salvation. It seems to me that only as we take what may be called the *sacramental* view of the Gospel, can we be justified in giving to it, as evangelical Protestantism does, the place of the most effective means of grace; through the physical acts of speaking and hearing the spiritual gifts of Christ as Saviour can be imparted to the soul. For the preacher this means humble and yet confident dependence upon God. Only as God's Spirit is given to him, so that in his speech Christ becomes real as the object of faith to his hearers, can he dare to hope that his preaching will be blessed to the saving of souls. His dependence, however, does not limit the preacher's liberty and responsibility. His is, with the Spirit's guidance and help, the liberty and the responsibility of the choice of the thoughts to be expressed, and the words for their expression. If his own vision of Christ is indistinct his presentation of Christ may be ambiguous. If his own conviction wavers he will not make others certain.

(b) Accordingly what the preacher needs first of all, and most of all is that he himself apprehend the Gospel, not as a form of words, but as this effective presentation of Christ Himself in His truth and grace to the faith of the hearers. If for the preacher Christ is not really presented, if for him the Spirit of God is not really acting to make men receptive of, and responsive to Christ, must not his preaching become but as " clanging brass or tinkling cymbal " ? In such conditions, even if there is human eloquence, can there be a demonstration of the Spirit ? A philosophical conception, or even a religious belief in the general immanence of God will not give the certainty which inspires confidence. There must be a Christian experience, similar to Paul's. The preacher must know not only the Jesus of history, but the Christ of faith as the Living Saviour and Lord. For him the revelation of God and the redemption of man must be so identified with, and so inseparable from, the person and the work of Christ, that for him God must ever be present in Christ, the apprehension of the living Christ giving a gracious saving content to the presence of God, and the historical reality of Jesus making more concrete the conception of the living Christ. The Gospels give content to the Gospel, and the Gospel presents God in Christ.

(c) It seems to me that if our experience is moulded by that recorded in the New Testament, this apprehension of the living Christ Himself will be known to be, not by solitary unsustained human endeavour, but by the operation of God's own Spirit in mind, heart, and will. The inspiration of the Bible is often so accepted as to exclude the realization that the Church, as human faith receives and responds to divine grace, may be an *inspired* society. The inspiration of prophets and apostles is often conceived as so exclusive that the believer dare not believe that he too may be inspired according to his faith. The operation of the Spirit in the preacher and in the hearers may be felt as a mood of spiritual exaltation; but that is not necessary to its reality. It is not always when the preacher has this feeling that he is proving the most effective instrument of the Spirit of God. It is sometimes when he is suffering intense humiliation of soul, that the Spirit is using him. Not according to our feelings, but according to our faith is the operation of the Spirit of God in us. But what every preacher must desire, pray for, and strive after is that he may be made " a vessel meet for the Master's use." What has been written already proves that the intellectual equipment of the preacher, and the social sympathies, must be as wide as the mental and practical needs of men, but his essential endowment for effective ministry is the faith that makes Christ as Saviour and Lord real and the Spirit's working mighty in his life and work.

(3) That the preacher should convey to his hearers his own sense of the reality of the supersensible is more necessary to-day than ever. Preachers of former generations could appeal to the Bible or to the Church as an authority to which reason and conscience must submit. For many to-day that authority is doubtful, or even challenged. If, as has been said, the Church was abandoned at the Reformation for the Bible, and now the Bible is being abandoned for Christ as the ultimate authority, how can Christ be so mediated to men that His authority will command submission ? It can only be by living " epistles, known and read of all men " (2 Cor. iii, 2). It is the Christian experience and character that effectively mediate Christ to many men. And in his preaching, in the sense of reality, sincerity, and intensity which is conveyed by it, the preacher can become a living epistle. More than ever, as Bishop Phillips Brooks stated,* in preaching truth must come through human personality.

* _Lectures on Preaching_, p. 5.
213

Another reason may be suggested. This is an age of science, when men want evidence, rely on experience, have an interest in psychology. These characteristics are recognized and their demands met in the preacher who knows and understands his own inner life, the presence of Christ in his experience, the operation of the Spirit of God in his personal development. A greater responsibility thus falls upon him, but also a greater privilege is accorded to him. He is not merely repeating what the Bible or the Church has told him to say; but he is testifying out of the reality of his own Christian spiritual life to the love of God in the grace of Christ by the communion of the Holy Spirit.

II. This insistence on the preacher's personal apprehension of the truth that he proclaims to others may appear a limitation of the pulpit, and exposure of it to the danger of subjectivity.

(1) It is a danger, for there are preachers of genius whose eccentricity gives too dominantly and even aggressively an individual character to their preaching. The preacher without genius may have developed his personality in so partial a way that only a fragmentary Gospel may find expression in his message. But would it be an advantage that he should supplement that Gospel by repetition at second-hand of truths that have not been translated for him out of thought into reality? Must not such preaching ring hollow to hearers with any spiritual sensitiveness? Surely better is a partial Gospel preached with conviction than a more adequate

Gospel preached without any conviction. Whatever is preached must be preached with absolute sincerity. But that lays on the preacher the duty of seeking ever to rise above and reach beyond his individual limitations to a personal apprehension of the whole Gospel, the Gospel adequate to meet the varied needs of his hearers. He must not only widen his intelligence by biblical and theological study so that he may enter on the rich inheritance of truth which is handed on in the Church from age to age; but he must also widen his own experience and character by the life of common fellowship and service that the Church, the community of the Spirit, offers him. It is by such means that he will make his own inner possession that Gospel in which grace abounds even beyond the measure of sin (Rom. v. 20).

(2) As one who from schoolboy days, now nearly for half a century, has been striving to apprehend for himself, and for more than forty years to present to others a Gospel which can be sincerely held, and fervently offered to others, may I venture to state the truths that it seems to me the Gospel adequate to human need must include? Despite the far-reaching changes in Christian theology which modern thought has brought about, there is far more of the Gospel which an intelligent and honest man can conserve than extremists on the one side or the other often lead young preachers especially to assume.

(a) The reality of sin does not depend on any theory of its origin. Social judgments on individual conduct, the law's dealing with crime, the conscience of each man bear witness that man has liberty and responsibility, and that he incurs blame or guilt by the abuse of that liberty. It is a disaster that for the common mind the need of Christ is associated with the fall of Adam, so that when the literal historical interpretation of Genesis iii is given up, it is often assumed that the Gospel has lost its contact with fact. It is often said that men have less sense of sin than they once had. May that not be due to Christian preachers failing to adjust their language to the new situation, and thus when they speak of sin conveying to their hearers the feeling of unreality? Both the psychological and the sociological approach to the facts of life, the development of the individual, and his relation to his fellows as a member of society will lead the morally sensitive man to apprehend afresh for himself the reality that sin with its evil consequences abounds. It may be that for many hearers the sociological approach will be more effective.

(*b*) There is a growing interest in the Social Problem; the social consciousness has been stimulated, and the social conscience has become more sensitive. We must recognize that there are world-wide factors in producing the present situation, and that, as it has not been produced directly by conscious, voluntary action, so it cannot be altered immediately by the amendment of individual lives. Nevertheless individual selfishness, greed, carelessness, lovelessness are largely responsible for social wrongs and miseries; and the preacher can challenge each man to examine himself whether his character and conduct are helping or hindering social progress. Again the motive of " self-reverence " the appreciation of the value of the human personality may be appealed to as challenging a man not only to self-knowledge but also to self-control. That by sin a man injures his whole self, and inflicts wrong on his fellows is a representation of sin that will for many hearers give a sense of reality.

(c) The relation of sin to God need not be passed over. But such a definition of sin as that of the Shorter Catechism that sin is " any transgression of, or want of conformity to the law of God," is for to-day too abstract. There is a law of God; but the analogy by which its reality should be brought home is not that of the human law-court, with its often arbitrary connection between offence and punishment, and its possibilities of evasion and escape, but that of the order of nature, where effect follows cause with an inescapable regularity. Of Paul's two metaphors: " The wages of sin is death " (Rom. vi. 23), and " He that soweth unto his own flesh shall of the flesh reap corruption; but he that soweth unto the Spirit shall of the Spirit reap eternal life " (Gal. vi. 8), there can be no doubt the second is the more effective to-day.

(d) It is on these same lines that the preacher should deal with future destiny. A Heaven or a Hell, depending on a divine sentence, has lost its attraction or its restraint. Let the preacher call attention to the continuity of character; and insist that what a man is making himself now, that he is making himself for the hereafter, as death cannot break the moral bond. The Indian idea of *Karma*, each successive life being the resultant of character and conduct in the preceding, with such modification as the recognition of divine grace and human freedom demands, is much nearer reality than the artificial connection which in popular preaching has often been presented as obtaining between the present and the future life. The assumption that final destiny is irrevocably fixed at death revolts the conscience, because the moral development of many is incomplete, whether for good or evil; and it is inconsistent with the faith in God's Fatherhood, whose holy love in its seeking to save cannot have so arbitrary a limit set to it. In life there are " mirror-moments " (James i. 23-25), as when Judas discovered that he had " betrayed innocent blood " (Matt. xxvii. 4), or when Peter saw the judgment of forgiving love in the look of Jesus (Luke xxii. 61), or when Paul saw the Jesus whom he was persecuting (Acts ix. 5). These moments may issue in a godly sorrow that is unto life as was Peter's, or a sorrow without hope as was that of Judas, which ends in death. Is it not reasonable to suppose that death may be such a mirror-moment, in which the soul sees itself in contrition or remorse, and lays hold on grace, or falls under judgment ?

(*e*) What may with all seriousness and urgency be insisted on is that the soul in this life, at death, or in the after-life fixes its own destiny as it accepts or refuses the saving grace of God. Sin in its ultimate development may be truly represented as not disobedience to God's law, but as distrust of His love. The final condemnation will fall, and cannot but fall on those who finally refuse the salvation that is in Christ Jesus, for this refusal is the soul's own self-disclosure. " This is the judgment that the light is come unto the world, and men loved the darkness rather than the light; for their works were evil " (John iii. 19). This judgment is being carried out here and hereafter. Can sin's heinousness be made more evident than where it is shown to be not only defiance of the thunders of Sinai, but refusal of the pleadings of Calvary? As in human relationships, the more intimate the relation the more the affection required and expected, and the more shameful and hurtful any lack of loyalty, or failure in fidelity. A man can sin more deeply against his wife than against a stranger. If God be not only Creator, Preserver, Ruler, and Lawgiver, but Father and in Christ Saviour, then sin against His love must deserve deeper condemnation than would even sin against His law. We must lift our treatment of sin into the region of personal relations, to self, to neighbour, and to God, to restore to men the sense of its reality, and consequently of the necessity for forgiveness.

(3) As we deal with the reality of sin, so must we treat the necessity for forgiveness. If God's forgiveness meant only the cancelling of the future penalty of sin, escape from Hell, and assurance of Heaven, then certainly the growing disbelief in eternal punishment would blunt the edge of the urgent appeal of the Christian Gospel. Forgiveness, how-

ever, defined very simply, is the restoration by divine grace on human penitence and faith of the personal relation between God and man disturbed by sin. On this the Christian preacher should concentrate.

(*a*) This does not necessarily involve an immediate arrest of the consequences, physical, social, personal, of the former life of sin. A man's health may continue bad; his reputation and influence among his fellow-men may not be recovered; the former temptations may still assail him; and the former habits hamper him in his new life, because, as was indicated in the previous paragraph, the connection of sin and its consequences is not arbitrary, imposed or removed by divine decree, as theology has sometimes represented. But forgiveness does involve a change in the whole life. We are learning now how much mind influences body, and so the man may become healthier as he turns from evil ways, and trusts in God. Although society is too distrustful of the new convert, and men do not emulate the generosity of God, yet a man who continues to show "the fruit of the Spirit" may recover his place among his fellows. The new relation to God brings a new standard, a new motive, and a new power into the soul; and so the man, if only slowly, becomes morally as well as religiously changed, and the religious experience is defective which does not result in the moral character. But even if the conditions of the life are not as fully changed as might be expected, the man who has really faith in God is changed towards his conditions. He bears contritely and humbly, without rebellion against God, or resentment towards man, or despair of self whatever of " the body of his former death " still cleaves to and hampers his new life. " All things work together for good to them that love God (Romans viii. 28): for theirs is the assurance that nothing can separate them from " the love of God which is in Christ Jesus our Lord" (ver. 39). Reconciled to God a man is reconciled to the world and to himself, to life and death, to the here and the hereafter. In all relations he is attaining " the peace of God which passeth all understanding."

(*b*) What does this reconciliation to God involve ? It means the removal of doubt and fear, distrust and estrangement in the relation of man to God, the sense of guilt, and the apprehension of judgment. It is not the discovery, as some misinterpreting the holy love of God appear to think, that there never was any occasion for this distress, because on God's side the relation had never been disturbed, that to the subjective sense of guilt in man there never corresponded any objective fact of guilt in the eyes of God, nor to the human apprehension any divine intention of judgment. It is a deadly error to charge God with moral indifference to, personal tolerance of, or compromise with sin and easy good nature that, unpained by sin, forgives sin without any cost of pain. So far as there is any ground for the complaint that many young people to-day are showing a lack of discipline, it may be traced to the parental error of so misconceiving God's Fatherhood. The consequences of sin, inevitable and not arbitrary, are an indication of God's judgment on sin. To call them natural is not to relieve God of ultimate responsibility for them, unless we erect an abstraction, *Nature*, as a reality between God and man. Nor is it conceivable that man's moral consciousness, in which man has closest affinity with God, should deceive him as to what is the real attitude of God to sin. In the sinner's attitude to God there is much that is subjective, fear, distrust, estrangement; but the sense of guilt and the apprehension of judgment surely carry their own evidence of objectivity. The saint loses these subjective feelings, but not that objective testimony to what the character and purpose of God are. God's forgiveness does involve the annulment of man's guilt, God's condemnation of his sin. If God be love, that condemnation is not an impassive judgment; it is sorrow, displeasure; dare we, in gazing on Christ's Cross, even say distress ?

(*c*) Accordingly it has always seemed to me to show a lack of moral and religious discernment to object to speaking about this reconciliation as mutual. Forgiveness means something to God as well as to man. It is not that God's disposition or purpose is changed; He is eternally holy love, and that love is not lost by sin, nor won again by man in forgiveness. But the outflow of God's good pleasure in man is held back by his sin, and set free by his penitence and faith. Sin puts restraint on the fulness and the freedom of His fellowship as Father with man as His child. It is true that the

New Testament speaks only of man's reconciliation to God; but if there be any mutuality in the personal relation of God and man, that surely presupposes God's reconciliation to man. In view of what Paul says in Romans iii. 25: " that God sets forth Christ as propitiatory " can we deny that God proclaims Himself reconciled ?

(4) According to the Gospel of the New Testament the forgiveness of sin comes to man by way of the atonement for sin in the death of Christ. (a) That Christ " died for our sins according to the Scriptures (1 Cor. xv. 3), was no less a part of the common tradition of the Christian Church from the beginning than that " He hath been raised on the third day according to the Scriptures " (ver. 4). Nevertheless there is probably no doctrine about which many preachers feel greater difficulty and keep more silent in the pulpit. There is no ecclesiastical dogma regarding the work of Christ as there is regarding the person. There have been many theories of the atonement; but what has satisfied one age has repelled another. Probably in the Protestant Confessions of the sixteenth century there was a greater measure of agreement than there had been before, or has been since. When Grotius set himself, however, to defend against heresy the orthodox doctrine, he himself was by his own argument led away from it. The doctrine has commanded the passionate devotion of some of the greatest minds of the Christian Church; and it has also provoked violent antagonism.

(*b*) The difficulty has sometimes been evaded by saying that we may believe the fact, although we have no theory; and the evasion has been rebuked by saying that the fact is meaningless without some theory. If by the fact is meant merely that Christ died, then that of course is an object of historical belief, and not of personal faith; but as soon as we add " for our sins " we put some meaning into the fact that calls for some explanation; *how* and *why* did He die for our sins? It seems to me we can put a great deal of moral and religious meaning into the fact by following up the *how*, even if we have to stop short at the *why*. Interpreting Gethsemane and Calvary in the light of what sin involves for holy love (in which human love at its best offers us some analogy to divine love) we may believe that Christ as the Son of God in His holy love for God judged sin as God judges it, and approved death as the expression of God's judgment on sin on the one hand; and that on the other hand He as Son of Man in His holy love for man felt the shame and sorrow of sin, and God's judgment on sin in death with and for man. One in his holy love with God and man, in His desolation on Calvary (anticipated in the agony of Gethsemane) there met in Him God's judgment on sin and man's endurance of that judgment. God as man in Christ's Cross endured His own judgment on man's sin. Jonathan Edwards and McLeed Campbell in their theories indicate this line of interpretation. As Christ was sinless, and never held Himself guilty, or was held guilty by God, it seems to me imperative that we should avoid all such words as punishment, confession, repentance, even if qualified by such words as substitutionary or vicarious, as that can lead only to moral confusion. The human conscience can approve, and I believe in the measure of its sensitiveness will approve, God's judgment on sin in its consequences however painful to self or to others. The human heart can appreciate the shame and the sorrow, which the endurance of these consequences may bring to a loved one as its very own. As Christ loved God and man perfectly, He experienced absolutely what even the best men can experience but partially. " He tasted death for every man " (Heb. ii. 9). It was in such an experience of God's judgment of sin in death, approved by Him as Son of God, endured by Him as Son of Man, that the love of God as the Father who forgives sin was conveyed to men. It is better to speak of the atonement in Christ's death as the conveyance of God's forgiveness than as the condition of it; as it does not separate the one from the other, but identifies them. A universal forgiveness of sin is offered to mankind, to be individually claimed by penitence and faith, in the very act in which God as man in Christ takes upon Himself His own universal judgment of the sin forgiven. In His grace God fully identifies Himself with " mankind sinners " in enduring the judgment of their sin, and in faith each man identifies himself with God in accepting by his own penitence that judgment of his sin. Thus the personal relation of God and man, interrupted by sin, is perfectly restored, for God endures, and man approves the judgment of sin, and thus the moral unity of God and man is recovered.

(c) It may be objected that this account of the *how* of Christ's death for our sins assumes that there is a divine judgment upon sin. I have already in the previous paragraph dealing with forgiveness met the objection; but I may here add that to me it is inconceivable that there should not be a divine judgment on sin. If my imperfect human conscience condemns sin in myself and others, how can the holy love of God do other than condemn sin? Incapable of logical demonstration, that is a fundamental moral intuition, the denial of which seems to me to challenge the moral nature and purpose of God Himself.

(d) If it be further objected that death is a physical necessity, and no divine judgment, my answer is that for man as an animal death may be a physical necessity; but the moral and religious content of death as a personal experience is something more. I cannot understand Christ's dread in Gethesemane or His distress on Calvary unless death was for Him something more. As death is apart from the hope which Christ gives, Paul seems to me to express one of these fundamental moral intuitions which no amount of reasoning can overthrow when he says that " the wages of sin is death " (Rom. vi. 23). Even if the final judgment of God on sin does not fall at death, as has been maintained in the previous discussion, man's forebodings in death anticipate such final judgment. For more than forty years

I have been pondering this problem, and I cannot escape the conviction that Christ's death meant for Him God's judgment on sin, and His endurance with and for man of that judgment. For Him the many could not be ransomed, the sacrifice of the new covenant of forgiveness and fellowship with God could not be accomplished, unless He died and died as He did with the cry of dereliction on His lips. What He accepted in Gethesemane as the cup which could not pass from Him was not death merely as physical dissolution (that He had accepted long before that hour), but death as divine judgment on the sin of man. As I read the records of the sacrifice of Christ His death meant nothing less, or other than this.

(5) When we pass from the *how* to the *why* of the death of Christ we cannot hope for the same measure of agreement. It is there that theories go apart; and their difference has been expressed by the terms *subjective* and *objective*. May we think only of the influence of His death on man in bringing man to penitence and faith by exhibiting the love of God unto self-sacrifice ? This was Abelard's theory, although in view of the teaching of Scripture he could not maintain it consistently, and had to make concessions to the other standpoint. Or must we think as well of the significance of the death for God, as most of the theories of the atonement have tried to do ? To this distinction itself objection may be made on the ground that, if there be moral affinity of God and man, and if the purpose of God in Christ was to restore the moral community of

God and man, then what influences man must surely
be also significant for God. Again, a sacrifice has
value as a proof of love only when it is necessary.
To make a sacrifice merely to show love is spectac-
ular, and not impressive. The death of Christ
could exercise a moral influence on man only as it
was the fulfilment of a moral obligation other than
the desire and intention to exercise such an influence.
What alone can make a moral impression on man,
adequate to effect that change in man without which
he cannot be reconciled to God, is the disclosure
that it is thus and only thus that God in His holy
love can forgive. It is the significance of the Cross
for God which alone can exercise its full influence
on man. It is a dangerous antithesis to oppose what
Christ does in man, and what He does in God.
But we may say that God discloses in Christ what
He Himself is, and wills in regard to sin; and only
by such a disclosure can man himself be brought
into the same attitude to sin as is God's. If this
attitude in man is necessary for his forgiveness,
this disclosure is no less necessary for God in
forgiving. God as holy love must no less disclose
His holiness than His love in forgiving, for His love
is but the communicativeness of His perfection.
It is then a necessity for God as moral perfection
communicating itself morally to man to convey His
judgment on sin in His forgiveness; and that the
death of Christ, as it has just been interpreted,
achieves as no other dealing of God with man could
do. The necessity for the death of Christ which
Paul suggests in Romans iii. 25, is that God needed

to vindicate His character as righteous against the
suspicion of moral indifference which His former
tolerance of sin might provoke. It is well for us
to remember that he was here arguing against
Pharisaic Judaism. Taking Christ's own revelation
of God as the perfect Father, as holy love, it is
better for us to find that necessity in the very nature
as well as the purpose towards men of that holy
love. If we knew sin as God knows it, and if our
love were holy as His is, we should surely understand this necessity. Here too logical demonstration is impossible; only moral and religious
discernment can serve. If a preacher cannot apprehend this necessity, as he feels his responsibility
for the souls of men, let him not deny it, even if
he cannot declare it. But if he can declare it, blessed
is he, for he will speak from the depths of God's
grace to the depths of man's needs.

III. In this chapter no attempt has been made
to discuss all that may be included in the preaching
of the Gospel. There are philosophical and theological implications, which the preacher must discuss
from the standpoint of modern thought; there are
practical, individual, and social applications which
he must assert in view of the needs of modern society;
there is the abundant treasure of illustration and
confirmation of the Gospel which the study of the
Bible by modern methods will yield. What this
chapter has alone sought to do, is to prove and urge
that, however wide may be the circumference of the
preacher's interests, the centre which is essential,
if his preaching is to be genuinely representative of

the Living Church and its creed, is Christ and Him
Crucified. Sin, Forgiveness, Atonement—these are
the keywords of the Gospel which "is not after
man," nor received "from man," but comes to
the preacher, as to Paul, "through revelation of
Jesus Christ," when it is "the good pleasure of
God to reveal His Son in him" (Gal. i. 12, 16).
Only as for the preacher "to live is Christ"
(Phil. i. 21) can he in his words become the voice
of Christ in His Living Church.

CONCLUSION

THE FUTURE OF PREACHING

THE Historical Section of this volume has shown how important has been the function, and how influential the personality of the preachers of the Church. The Practical Section has endeavoured to show what is the demand of the modern world upon the preacher, and how it can be met. In closing it seems desirable to glance at some of the signs of the times, the indications of what the future of preaching is likely to be.

I. There is a widespread opinion that the day of preaching is done. It is held on the one hand that worship is superseding and will still more supersede preaching, and on the other hand that the place of preaching can be taken by other means of conveying the truth to the minds of men.

(*a*) The remark is not uncommon that people go to church to worship God, and not to hear a man talk. Such a contrast is unreal. " How then shall they call on him on whom they have not believed ? and how shall they believe in him whom they have not heard ? and how shall they hear without a preacher ? " (Romans x. 14). The foundations of the Christian Church were laid by the preaching

231

of Jesus and of His apostles; and the structure of the Church, as we have seen, has been again and again repaired, when it seemed to be falling in ruins, by the preachers whom God has raised up. Devotion depends on conviction, and conviction on testimony. When the Gospel is not preached and believed, worship becomes a soulless routine. Again, preaching is worship. If in worship there is a mutual communion of God and man, God's speaking to man is not less, but more important than man's speaking to God. If preaching be "truth through personality," the preacher is to be blamed who allows his personality to be more prominent than is the truth. If the preacher, however, always thinks of himself as God's messenger, and seeks to discover and deliver only God's message, then it is not a man who is talking, but God who is speaking by man. "How shall they preach except they be sent? Even as it is written, How beautiful are the feet of them that bring glad tidings of good things!" (ver. 15). It is not a contrite, humble, modest piety which will depreciate the preaching of the Gospel.

(b) In the review of a book on preaching the opinion was confidently stated that people would more and more prefer to read than to hear sermons, and that consequently the literary quality of the sermon must be the first consideration. This shows an entire misunderstanding of the capacity and the inclination of the majority of human beings. It is the personality that in preaching most effectively mediates the truth. Putting the fact in biological terms, man is a gregarious animal; or using the words of philosophy, he develops individually, not apart from, but in society. The spoken word makes an appeal which the written word cannot, and the written word has an added attraction if the writer is known and has been heard. The personal knowledge helps in the appreciation of the word as read. The immediate contact of one personality with another makes an impression such as the most careful study of a book cannot. Further there is the influence in preaching not only of the preacher, but of the congregation. There is a spiritual stimulus in a worshipping community, such as private meditation and devotion does not command, at least not with most persons. On this ground at least preaching will not be superseded by reading. Nor, it may be added, even by the broadcasting of services and sermons on Sunday evenings. If the sermon is to be spoken, and not read, another test must be supplied than literary quality. What could be appreciated in the quiet of study might be quite ineffective if heard only in a church. The sermon, even when the preacher himself reads it, must be composed, not as an essay but as a speech.

(c) There is still another danger to which the pulpit of to-day seems to be exposed. In a weekly political journal some years ago appeared the statement that the writer of the article, as soon as a preacher became eloquent, began to suspect him as a humbug. We cannot, and would not restore the artificial and sometimes pompous oratory of the past; but the tendency is being carried too far in public speaking to suppress imagination and passion, and to speak in very plain prose with as little show of feeling as possible. All unreality is an abomination, most of all in the pulpit, the sincerity of which must never be laid bare to suspicion; but the themes with which the preacher deals—the tragedy of sin, the triumph of the Cross, the glory of life eternal, all that sounds the abysmal depths of man, and scales the sublime heights of God—must surely inspire eloquence, the vivid imagination, and the intense emotion. Self-restraint there must be, but the pulpit will surely lose much of its advantage if the preacher unduly suppresses his own personality, his vision and his passion. Egotism must be shunned as a plague; but the preacher must put his whole self at the disposal of God, so that through his wholly consecrated personality the truth shall convince and convert.

II. It is probably the depreciation of preaching which is in some measure responsible for the steady decrease in the numbers of those who offer themselves for the Christian ministry.

(*a*) If the need for, and the power of preaching in the Church is rated lower than other activities of Christian service, if the layman's contribution to the thought and life of the Church is deemed just as valuable as the minister's, it is much less likely that young men will believe themselves called of God; or if their inclinations lie that way will regard the call as so imperative that obedience to it will not only justify, but constrain the personal sacrifices which are involved. Only if there is a recovery of the sense of urgency for the delivery of the Christian Gospel as a task which God Himself lays on those whom He has chosen, only if the sacredness of the vocation of the preacher as God's messenger is again asserted, only if this calling is exalted above any other which can satisfy aspiring youth, will the Church secure the number and the quality of the preachers whom the world's need demands. Comparatively few of the young men of greatest ability and highest distinction in the Universities offer themselves for the ministry at home or abroad; only a small number come from the well-to-do or wealthy homes. Even Christian parents are found who judge that they can do best for their sons in some other profession. We must not be rash or harsh in condemning this judgment as selfish and worldly. Is the minister of Christ so esteemed in the Church, to say nothing of the world, that the young man or his parents would be constrained to feel sorrowfully that there had been " the great refusal," if given the capacity, the education, and the inclination, the call of the ministry were unheard, or unheeded ? The future of preaching depends on getting the best in capacity and character for this calling; and getting the best does not depend so much on individual persuasion, as on a general attitude both of the ministers and the members of the churches. The Church which thinks, feels, and wills the best for its ministry will get its best as ministers.

(*b*) Two other hindrances to securing young men for the ministry may be mentioned, although they are subordinate. With a few exceptions the ministers are far worse paid than men of like ability or education in any other profession. It would be a disaster if the ministry were made financially as attractive as the other professions. It is well that some disadvantages should attach to it, so that the worldly may be kept away from it. But privation and anxiety should not be needlessly inflicted. The preacher should be freed at least from earthly care that he may, undistracted and undisturbed, devote himself with his whole mind, and soul, and strength, to his heavenly task. More serious an obstacle is the fear of intellectual, moral, and spiritual bondage in the ministry. A man may fulfil his calling despite privation and anxiety about temporal things, but how can he fulfil that calling, if he is not allowed freedom to speak and to act as the Spirit of God will bid him ? If the traditions and conventions, the prejudices and ignorances of his congregation are allowed to set bounds to his service of the Gospel and the Kingdom, how can he dare to undertake a task that he will not be allowed to discharge ? In preceding chapters it has been shown how imperative it is that the preacher shall adapt, if not the essential content of his message, yet the immediate presentation of it to the needs and claims of his age and his surroundings. He can be the voice of a Living Church only as he has freedom to grow himself. The future of preaching depends on the fit and worthy preacher being fully trusted to use, and not abuse, his freedom.

III. If the preacher is to use his freedom worthily, he must be properly trained. From what has been said in the preceding chapters it is evident how wide must be the range of his interests, and how varied his activities. But this consideration may lead to a false conclusion and a wrong application.

(a) The demand is sometimes made that the theological college shall teach every subject of which the preacher may need to have knowledge to do his work effectively; and preachers are sometimes heard complaining that they were not taught at college some subject to which the attention of the Church was not directed till many years after their course was completed. The improved methods of Sunday School teaching were comparatively a novelty a generation ago. The challenge of the Social Problem was not realized till the latter half of last century. All that can be required is that the college shall not lag behind in making provision for the recognized needs of the ministry. Not every preacher is concerned with the whole range of problems, intellectual, moral, social, spiritual with which the Church as a whole is confronted. Local and even temporary conditions affect the kind of challenge that the Christian pulpit must be ready to meet. The social problem will be presented in different aspects in an agricultural and an industrial district. In some congregations the intellectual difficulties of the Christian faith will be more acutely felt than in others. The legitimate demand upon the college is that it shall give such a training as will in each student develop as fully as possible his individual capacity, so that he will know how to study any subject to which the demands of his pulpit direct his interest. It cannot attempt to teach all that it may be profitable for a preacher to know; but it is bound to train him to study. We need not stop short at this general statement, as the kind of training may in some respects be more exactly defined.

(*b*) It is evident that the preacher must on the one hand know the Bible so as to use it most effectively, and the Gospel so as to present it most persuasively; and on the other hand he must know the needs he is called to meet. A defect which it must be frankly admitted has prevailed and persisted in theological colleges has been that too often attention has been so exclusively given to meet the first demand as to involve the neglect of the second. A Biblical scholar should certainly have command over the original tongues in which the literature of revelation was written; and a theologian should know the history of Christian doctrines within the Church. But the preacher, unless he has the capacity and inclination, need not be a scholar and a theologian in the technical sense; but may be trained so to present the truth as it is in Jesus as " to win souls for his hire," even although he does not know the minutiæ of Hebrew grammar, or the subtleties of the creeds. What is wanted is more elasticity and more adaptation to individual capacity. The mental discipline must be rigorous enough to develop fully mental capacity; but that discipline may be secured by the study of other than the subjects which tradition has prescribed. The linguistic demands—Latin, Greek and Hebrew—of the course usually required are so severe on some students that their study becomes a bondage to them, and their development is not furthered, but hindered. While on the one hand these demands seem justified if the preacher is to be thoroughly qualified as an interpreter of the Bible and an exponent of the Gospel, to meet them fully is perforce to exclude other studies which seem no less necessary, if he is to understand the world to which he is to be God's messenger. It seems necessary here to emphasize what the usually accepted curriculum has tended to ignore—that the preacher must have full knowledge and keen understanding of his own age, its problems and its resources. To teach him the sins of the house of Israel and not the wrongs around him is surely to fail in giving the preacher the training that he needs. Room must be found for studies which hitherto have been ignored. But whatever newer subjects are included, care must be taken to teach them with the thoroughness with which the older subjects have been taught, so that they afford a rigorous discipline for the mind. The " tit-bits " kind of curriculum, which is being adopted in some colleges that aim at being very modern, is an injury to the mind of the student. But science and scholarship are being applied to these modern problems; there is no reason why sociology should not be as good a means of mental development as metaphysics, or a knowledge of the twentieth century not be as scholarly as a knowledge of the first. By whatever method it is achieved, what is essential is that the preacher should not be out of touch with the thought and life around him, but at home in it, so that he can speak from his own heart to the hearts of all who hear. Hence theological colleges should not be little gardens walled round and apart; but in as close connection with the wider interests of thought which a university cultivates, and in the full current of the manifold life and work of the great city. His training must not make the preacher a doctrinaire or a recluse.

(c) God has graciously not given us the gift of seeing what good or ill the future may hold, unless such foresight of the immediate future as our insight into the present, out of which the future is emerging, allows. But if the history of the past or the experience of the present warrants, as it does, the expectation for the future that the Christ will avail for to-morrow as He has availed for yesterday and is availing for to-day, and that it is by the testimony and influence of the Church as His body that He will continue to speak and to work until God's purpose through Him is fulfilled, then we can rest assured that God will raise up, call, and equip His own messengers through whom the Jesus Christ who is " the same yesterday, to-day, and for ever " will speak " all the days unto the consummation of the age."

INDEX

INDEX

INDEX

243

INDEX

INDEX

BRISTOL : BURLEIGH LTD., AT THE BURLEIGH PRESS

"THE HUMANISM OF THE BIBLE" SERIES

EDITED BY

Professor JOHN EDGAR McFADYEN,
B.A., (Oxon.) D.D.

(*United Free Church College, Glasgow*)

AND

Professor D. RUSSELL SCOTT, M.A., Ph.D.

(*Congregational College, Edinburgh*)

Crown 8vo, cloth boards, 6s. net per volume.
Or the Set of 16 Volumes complete for £4 5s.

The aim of the Series is to set forth the human experience that underlies, and is reflected in, the Bible. The doctrinal and theological treatment of the Bible has undoubtedly tended to obscure its transcendent human interest. This series is an attempt to recover some of those ancient experiences and personalities which come to expression in the Bible, and to show how fascinating and relevant they are to the life of to-day. It seeks in a broad way to interpret the spirit of the Biblical books with which it deals, and to indicate their permanent human interest and worth.

" If the series may be judged by its first volume, it promises to fulfil admirably its purpose of making the Bible a more human book."—*Glasgow Herald*.

THE HIDDEN ROMANCE OF THE NEW TESTAMENT. By PROF. JAMES ALEX. ROBERTSON, D.D., Author of " The Spiritual Pilgrimage of Jesus," etc. Fourth Impression, 6s. net.

" He makes the New Testament more human, more real, more intelligible to the modern mind, and this in these days is a service of the greatest value."—*The Record*.

" Prof. Robertson has produced a work of enthralling interest, and one that fully justifies its title."—*Methodist Times*.

ALTARS OF EARTH. Studies in Old Testament Humanism. By HUBERT L. SIMPSON, M.A., Author of " The Intention of His Soul." Second edition. 6s. net.

" The buoyancy and vigour of his style, with the robust and positive religious thinking, should make this book as popular as it is strong and healthy."—*Glasgow Herald*.

" This is a remarkable book. It compels the reader to turn back to the Bible, and to read the Book of Genesis again."—*Dundee Courier*.

THE BEAUTY OF THE BIBLE. A Study of its Poets and Poetry. By Prof. James Stalker, D.D. Second edition. 6s. net.

" There is more information in these lucidly written pages than the general reader is likely to gain from more technical books. Dr. Stalker has, in fact, here contributed one of the most attractive volumes to the ' Humanism of the Bible ' series."—*The Times*

GOD IN HISTORY. By Professor James Strahan, M.A., D.D. Author of " Hebrew Ideals," " The Book of Job Interpreted," etc. 6s. net.

" Depth of insight, freshness of phrase, happy literary allusion, all combine to make the book most helpful to preachers and to all who really desire to understand the positive contribution of the Old Testament to our modern faith."—*The British Weekly.*

THE FELLOWSHIP OF THE SPIRIT. By Charles A. Anderson Scott, M.A., D.D. (Camb.), Hon.D.D. (Aberd.), Westminster College, Cambridge, Author of " Jesus and Paul," " The Book of Revelation," etc. 6s. net.

" This book is marked by freshness and independence and should not be neglected by students of the Apostolic Church."—*Holborn Review.*

THE FAITH OF ISAIAH. Statesman and Evangelist. By Alex. R. Gordon, D.Litt., D.D., Professor of Hebrew, McGill University, and of Old Testament Literature and Exegesis, Presbyterian College, Montreal. 6s. net.

" There should be room for this compact and forcibly written volume."—*Church Times*

" We commend the book for its intrinsic interest as well as for its value as an introduction to Isaiah."—*Christian World.*

JESUS AND LIFE. By Joseph F. McFadyen, M.A., D.D., Professor of New Testament Literature and Exegesis, Queen's University, Kingston, Canada. Fourth impression. 6s. net.

" It will be ranked with Glover's ' The Jesus of History ' as a fine example of present-day apologetic. . . . It is admirably fitted to guide and strengthen thoughtful men in the present hour and under the present strain."—*Glasgow Herald.*

THE INCARNATE GLORY. An Expository Study of the Gospel according to St. John. By William Manson, D.D., Professor at New College, Edinburgh, Author of " Christ's View of the Kingdom of God," etc. 6s. net.

" The book is finely written, balanced and sane, and worthy of a wide sale. Prof. Manson is to be congratulated on this excellent volume."—*Edinburgh Evening News.*

THE PROBLEM OF PAIN. A Study in the Book of Job. By Professor J. E. McFadyen, D.D. Second edition. 6s. net.

" An exceedingly clever and original study in the Book of Job. The author throws fresh light on the tragic Old Testament story, and his new rhythmical renderings of many passages in the book are particularly striking."—*Sheffield Daily Telegraph.*

ORACLES OF GOD. Studies in the Minor Prophets. By W. E. ORCHARD, D.D., Author of " Sermons on God, Christ and Man," " Advent Sermons," etc. 6s. net.

" It would be difficult to find a more readable or more intelligible introduction to the study of this important and too much neglected section of the Holy Scriptures."— *Nottingham Journal.*

PESSIMISM AND LOVE IN ECCLESIASTES AND THE SONG OF SONGS, with Translations from the same. By PROFESSOR DAVID RUSSELL SCOTT, M.A., Ph.D. 6s. net.

" An able and exhaustive analysis and explanation of Ecclesiastes. The book teems with valuable instruction for men of to-day."—*Liverpool Courier.*

THROUGH ETERNAL SPIRIT. A Study of Hebrews, James and I Peter. By JOSEPH F. McFADYEN, M.A., D.D., Professor of New Testament Language and Literature in Queen's Theological College, Kingston, Canada, Author of " Jesus and Life." 6s. net.

" A book like this would be an invaluable guide to a preacher bent on carrying his congregation through any or all of these three Epistles, which represent such diverse aspects of early Christian thought."—*Expository Times.*

THE PROPHET OF RECONSTRUCTION (Ezekiel). A Patriot's Ideal for a New Age. By W. F. LOFTHOUSE, M.A., Tutor in Hebrew Language and Literature, Handsworth College, Birmingham, Author of " Ethics and Atonement." 6s. net.

" A singularly fascinating book, which will enable many to give a tardy recognition to this great, solitary, brooding prophet, to whom his nation—and thus the world—owe so great a debt."—*Christian World.*

STUDIES IN LIFE FROM JEWISH PROVERBS. By PROFESSOR W. A. L. ELMSLIE, M.A., Cambridge. Second impression.

" A work of special interest. . . . Mr. Elmslie possesses much learning. . . . The book is full of good things, and will help any intelligent reader to understand books which, though they attract nearly everybody, often miss their aim because the reader cannot bring himself into anything like a living relation to their authors' experience." —*Times Literary Supplement.*

THE INDIVIDUALITY OF S. PAUL. By R. H. STRACHAN, D.D. Second impression. 6s. net.

" A close and careful investigation of the teaching of the Apostle. Mr. Strachan's style is crisp and pointed."—*The Times.*

THE BURDEN OF THE LORD. Aspects of Jeremiah's Personality, Mission and Age. By W. R. THOMSON, B.D., Author of " The Christian Idea of God," etc. 6s. net.

" This volume is a storehouse of information on the life and ministry of the one man who stood firm and faithful in days of vacillation, religious doubt, and lack of faith." —*Liverpool Courier.*

JAMES CLARKE & CO LTD., 9 ESSEX STREET, STRAND, LONDON W.C.2